smart soups

over 100 healthy & delicious recipes

Carol Heding Munson

Sterling Publishing Co., Inc.
New York

Acknowledgments

A hearty thank-you to Russell and Roger, who sampled every recipe and enthusiastically offered opinions. And a loving thank-you to Lowell for collaborating on the recipes and manuscript. His creativity and support made this book possible.

Library of Congress Cataloging-in-Publication Data Available

10 9 8 7 6 5 4 3 2 1

Published by Sterling Publishing Company, Inc.
387 Park Avenue South, New York, N.Y. 10016
©1998 by Carol Heding Munson
Distributed in Canada by Sterling Publishing
℅ Canadian Manda Group, One Atlantic Avenue, Suite 105
Toronto, Ontario, Canada M6K 3E7
Distributed in Great Britain and Europe by Cassell PLC
Wellington House, 125 Strand, London WC2R 0BB, England
Distributed in Australia by Capricorn Link (Australia) Pty Ltd.
P.O. Box 6651, Baulkham Hills, Business Centre, NSW 2153, Australia

Contents

Introduction

Soup's on! A slightly outdated expression, I suppose, but it's guaranteed to start your mouth watering, isn't it? Why? Soup's a wonderful soul-warming food that brims with wholesome ingredients and fantastic flavors. Indeed, soup's the epitome of comfort food. How many other dishes have the reputation for perking you up when a cold or the flu has you feeling down? What's more, soup fills you up. Yet, because it can be healthfully light in fat and calories, soup can be a dieter's best friend.

There are more reasons why soup holds a special place in our menu repertoire. A delicate, fragrant soup that stimulates the appetite makes for an enticing opener to an elegant dinner. By contrast, a robust soup, served with a crusty whole grain bread or a light salad, can make a satisfying, stick-to-the-ribs one-dish meal. The culinary reality is: soup's in; soup's hip.

Even so, do you shy away from making soup for one of these reasons? It takes too much cooking time—rumor has it at about eight hours of simmering. It requires too big a pot—a humongous one that holds 10 or 12 quarts. It calls for unique culinary skills. Well, I can assure you that neither all-day simmering nor space-gobbling equipment is necessary. As for the skills, if you can peel a potato and boil water, you can stir up a pot of splendid soup.

In this book, you'll see recipes for a wide variety of soups: some ready to eat in just an hour or so; some ready in mere minutes. Some have international origins; some are decidedly domestic. You'll need nothing larger than a 3- or 4-quart pot for soups, and an 8-quart pot if you prepare your own soup stocks. Most of these recipes make 4 or 6 servings—just the right amount for today's smaller families.

Ready to simmer up a potful of soup? Now is the perfect time, and here are more than 100 delicious recipes to choose from, including accompaniments.

Secrets to Making Superb Soups

It's 5:00 p.m., an hour before dinner at your place, and your mouth is watering for a comforting homemade soup. After all, it's been a crazy, hectic day, and now you'd like to unwind with something that has the power to soothe your soul and perk up your mood. Something to share with family or friends. Soup is the only answer.

But, you wonder, can you simmer up a soup—any soup: hot or cold, thick, thin, chunky, or smooth—in so little time? You bet your saucepan you can. I'm not talking about heating up an all-taste-alike canned or dehydrated concoction. And I'm not talking about high-tailing it to the deli for an offering that's laced with fat and sodium to mask a poorly made soup. I am talking about making a real, honest-to-goodness homemade soup, such as a light and delicate French onion soup, a rough-and-tumble chili soup, or a rustic chicken chowder. My "souper" speed trick: good commercial broth and beans to jump-start the process and small, uniformly cut pieces of foods for fast cooking. The flavor magic will come from ingredients blended on your stovetop.

And there's more quick goodness to homemade soups. Many are hearty enough to make complete meals—accompaniments such as crusty breads, crisp salads, and yummy desserts are options to be played when there's time. Remember: Most soups are one-pot affairs, so cleanup is a snap, and there's plenty of time to savor the satisfaction.

Are you ready, then, to throw together a superior soup in less than an hour? I'll help you get started with practical, easy-to-follow information on soup-making equipment, seasonings, garnishes, storing, and reheating.

BASIC TOOLS

You can create any of the soups in this book with just a few basic kitchen tools—none of which is high-tech or specialized. These are some of items I find especially useful.

Cutting board: At least one board in either plastic or wood is a must-have. Whichever you choose, be sure to get one that's large enough for unhindered chopping and small enough for easy washing by hand or in your dishwasher. My favorite size is about 11 x 15 inches. For food safety, remember to use separate boards (or separate sides of one board) for cutting vegetables and raw meats, and to wash the boards thoroughly between uses. When the boards become badly crisscrossed with cuts, it's time to replace them.

Chef's knife: This hefty knife, which comes in 6-, 8-, 10-, and 12-inch lengths, lets you cut meats, chop vegetables, and mince garlic and herbs in no time flat. The 8-inch one gets my vote for versatility, though some cooks prefer the 6- or 10-inch variety. Select a top-quality knife, and keep it sharp for great fast-track performance.

Paring knife: I use a paring knife with a 3-inch blade to make short work of trimming mushrooms; peeling apples, pears, and garlic; and similar tasks. These knives also come in a 4-inch size, if you prefer something just a little longer. Buy a quality product and sharpen it often for easy cutting. A sharp knife is always safer than a dull one.

Vegetable peeler: This simple tool is ideal for peeling thin-skinned root vegetables like carrots, potatoes, and parsnips. Some cooks also find them useful for peeling items such as cucumbers and young butternut squash. For no-hassle peeling, be sure to get a peeler with a sharp swivel blade and a fat, comfortable handle.

Measuring cups and spoons: You could use the guess 'n' create method, but using measuring cups and spoons will produce more consistent results. And besides, the cost of cups and spoons is quite reasonable. Get a nested set of dry measuring cups for measuring beans, pasta, rice, frozen peas and corn, and other similar ingredients. Use a liquid measure for broth, tomatoes, and other liquidy ingredients. The same set of nested spoons can be used for dry or moist items.

Large spoons: The marketplace has tons of different spoons available. These are the ones I like best:

Wooden spoons: I prefer these plain, old-fashioned utensils over metal and plastic varieties for most mixing and stirring tasks. Here's why: They don't scratch pots, pans, or dishes; and their shallow bowls are perfectly suited to stirring. What's more, their handles stay cool, and they don't melt if you accidentally leave them touching a hot pot. Handles come in short, medium, and long. My favorite length: medium. Since wooden spoons are inexpensive, I usually keep 3 or 4 handy.

Large metal spoon: A good-sized spoon with a deep bowl is ideal for serving hearty, chunky soups. Choose a plastic variety if you're concerned about scratching the interior of your saucepan or pot.

Just be aware that most plastic varieties stain easily, especially when exposed to tomatoes or turmeric.

Ladle: A ladle with a half-cup capacity is ideal for serving the lighter soups and chowders in this book. Select either plastic, ceramic, or metal.

3-quart saucepan or 4-quart pot: Why is one of these vessels called a saucepan and the other a pot? The smaller of the two has but one handle so it's called a saucepan; the larger has two handles and is, therefore, a pot. Any of the recipes in this book can be made in either the 3- or 4-quart vessel. The pot, however, will give you more room for stirring and gentle simmering. If you need to buy something, get a pot that has securely attached handles and a snug-fitting lid. The pot itself should be heavy; a nonstick interior is helpful, but not necessary.

Immersion blender: This handy gadget, which allows you to puree ingredients right in the pot, isn't a necessity, but it certainly speeds the process of making thick, creamy soups. If you don't have one, you'll need a blender, food processor, food mill, or potato masher instead to puree the ingredients for the creamy soups in this book. Make sure your immersion blender is designed for pureeing hot foods and that its shaft is fairly long.

Spice grinder: I love the way freshly ground spices punch up the flavor of soups and chowders. Get one of these gizmos (they're fairly inexpensive) if you'd like to grind your own spices, a practice I recommend since freshly ground spices have more flavor than preground varieties.

FLAVORING UP

If you've ever had a soup that left you flat, made your taste buds cry dullsville, then you know why I'm big on using herbs and spices. Both give foods jazz, pizzazz and special character, uniqueness and depth of flavor. And they give cuisines signature flavors. Imagine, if you will, Italian foods without basil or oregano, Mexican dishes sans cumin, Hungarian entrées minus paprika. Not much to tease and delight your taste buds, is there?

The herbs and spices called for in this book are readily available in the aisles of most supermarkets. There, you'll usually find everything from bay leaves and white pepper to exotic-sounding Chinese five-spice powder, Thai seasoning, herbes de Provence and Italian herb seasoning. So you needn't dig out those mail-order catalogs or traipse to either gourmet or ethnic markets, both of which can take valuable time.

Dried herbs and spices provide top flavor when they're young and lively, not old and weary from sitting on the shelf too long. So always buy seasonings in small quantities (those new half-size jars available in some markets are perfect) and replace them often. How frequently is that? Any dried herb and many preground spices more than a year old have lost much of their flavor power and are ready for retirement.

When storing dried herbs and spices, stash them in a cool, dry, dark spot. Unfortunately, those attractive spice racks that hang on sun-drenched kitchen walls make better decorations than storage places for seasonings.

Before using dried herbs, crush the leaves between your fingers to release their fragrance and flavor. Crush, grate or grind whole spice seeds, such as mustard seeds and peppercorns immediately before use. Freshly ground spices have greater impact than preground varities, which invariably lose their flavor during storage.

As mentioned before, freshly dried herbs have tons more flavor than older, tired ones. But what about fresh herbs? Their heavenly scent and intriguing flavor surpasses that of the dried variety, hands down, so I strongly urge you to seek fresh, whenever you can. Fresh herbs will keep in plastic bags in your refrigerator for several days. When fresh herbs aren't available, remember that fresh and dried are interchangeable in most soup recipes. This is the substitution equation: *1 tablespoon fresh herbs = 1 teaspoon dried herbs.*

While there's no right or wrong time to add herbs and spices to soups, certain times seem to bring out flavors better than others. As a general rule, this is what works for most soups in this book:

- Add spices near the beginning of cooking. Here's why: The concentrated, robust flavors of spices, which are the pungent roots, barks, stems, buds, fruits, and, sometimes, leaves of tropical and subtropical plants, benefit from cooking. The exceptions are black pepper and white pepper, which lose their snap when cooked too long.

- Stir in herbs near the end of cooking. The light flavor of herbs, which are the delicate leaves of plants that grow in temperate climes, dissipates easily in heat. But there are exceptions to this guideline, too: Rosemary and thyme, two rather intensely flavored herbs, are best added near the beginning.

What if you accidentally overseason a soup? Remain calm. Here are four rescues worth a try:

- Use a spoon to remove as much of the spice as possible, if you haven't stirred it all in as yet.

- Stir in a teaspoon of sugar to counteract a bitter, biting flavor.
- Add a quartered, peeled raw potato to the soup and simmer the mixture for 10 to 15 minutes. The potato will soak up some of the excess spicing. Discard the potato pieces.
- Make up a second batch of soup without seasonings. Combine the two batches to dilute the seasonings.

Broth Base. Though not a seasoning as such, a flavorful stock or broth has a tremendous impact on the taste of any homemade soup. In the recipes here, use a homemade stock, seasoned canned broth, or undoctored canned broth. Any of them will give your soup a flavorful foundation.

DRESSING UP

It's easy to dismiss garnishes as something frivolous, something extra—something fancy done only by chefs in trendy restaurants. Whoa, don't be so fast to ignore these snips, shreds, sprinkles and dollops. Garnishes can enliven almost any soup, making both its flavor and color practically pop out of the bowl. Here are some speedy and simple garnishes that make soups special.

Bacon: cooked until crisp and crumbled

Basil: fresh or dried, whole or snipped leaves

Black pepper: freshly ground

Caraway seeds

Cheese: any flavor, crumbled, grated, or shredded

Chives: fresh, dried, or frozen, snipped

Cilantro: fresh or dried, whole or snipped leaves

Croutons: plain or garlic

Lemon, lime, or orange: sliced or cut into wedges

Nuts: slivered, sliced, ground and toasted

Paprika: sprinkled

Parsley: fresh or dried, whole or snipped leaves

Scallions: bias sliced

Sour cream: swirled in

Yogurt: swirled in

FAST TRACK

Okay, I've said that soupmaking is 1-2-3 fast and easy. And it is. Still, a little organization will zap potential hassle factors. Here's what to organize:

The table. Start by setting the table. Put out the cups, plates, silverware, and serving dishes. By doing this first, you won't have to rush when the cooking is done.

Your thoughts. Begin by reading the recipe from start to finish. Make sure you understand the directions and reread any confusing instructions.

The ingredients. Start by getting out the required ingredients, and place them within fingertip reach. Then do all the slicing, dicing, and measuring, and place the prepared ingredients in small bowls and cups or in piles on waxed paper. To save washing the cutting board or food-processor bowl between items, chop dry ingredients, such as bread crumbs, first. Next slice moist ones, such as onions. Finally, cut meats or poultry. Return extra ingredients to the pantry, refrigerator, or freezer. Now, put everything together, and simmer up a great soup!

FOR ANOTHER TIME

A soup that makes enough for a second meal. That's what I call a super idea and time saver. Many recipes in this book can be doubled, and extra portions can be stashed in the refrigerator or freezer for enjoyment another time. Just be aware that some soups, such as the following, require special handling.

Soups with pasta in a flavor-rich broth. *Problem:* As the soup cools in the refrigerator or freezer, the pasta continues to absorb moisture. *Result:* Soggy, not al dente, pasta. *Easy fix:* Stir the pasta into each batch as you heat it for serving.

Chowders with potatoes. *Problem:* Potatoes don't freeze well. *Result:* Potatoes with mealy texture after thawing. *Easy fix:* Either add cooked potatoes to the soup as you prepare a batch for serving, or eliminate them from the recipe.

Chowders with milk. *Problem:* Milk-based soups will keep in the refrigerator for a day or two, but don't freeze well. They must be carefully heated so they don't boil. *Result:* Curdled milk when thawed or boiled. *Easy fix:* Reserve the milk, and add it when reheating the chowder.

10

When storing extra portions, remember to chill them as soon as possible. Food safety experts recommend refrigerating or freezing foods within 2 hours of cooking. I prefer a greater margin of safety and shoot for an hour or less. Really, there's no need for food to rest on the counter for several hours.

To reheat a soup, thaw it either in the refrigerator or microwave. Then, heat it on the stove top or in the microwave until it's bubbly hot through and through. Depending on the amount, reheating can take from 10 to 40 minutes—even longer if the amount of soup serves many.

CALORIES, FAT, AND OTHER NUTRITIONAL FACTS

Keeping an eagle eye on your intake of calories, fat, sodium, and fiber? Then you've come to the right book. Here I've provided a nutritional breakdown for each recipe. The analyses were done using a computer program called Nutritionist IV by First Data Bank and were calculated for single servings. If you prefer larger or smaller portions, though, you'll be taking in proportionally more or less nutrients.

Soup Stocks

Beef Stock

A lean stock that's rich and flavorful.

Yields: 9 cups

nonstick spray

2 ribs from roasted beef rib roast

2 celery stalks, leaves included, halved

4 large onions, with skins, quartered

4 medium carrots, halved

2 small turnips, quartered

2 bay leaves

8 whole black peppercorns

1 sprig parsley

1 sprig rosemary

10 cups water

Coat a nonstick skillet with the spray and warm it over medium-high heat for 1 minute. Add the beef ribs and cook them until the pieces are browned on all sides. Transfer the ribs to an 8-quart pot. Add the celery, onions, carrots, turnips, bay leaves, peppercorns, parsley, rosemary, and water. Cover the pot, and bring the mixture to a boil. Reduce the heat, and simmer for 2 hours.

Pour the stock through a large strainer into a large bowl or pot. Discard the beef bones, vegetables, and seasonings. Chill the stock; then skim and discard the fat that's accumulated on the top of the liquid.

Per cup: 47 calories, 1 g fat, 0 g saturated fat, 0 mg cholesterol, 70 mg sodium, 0 g dietary fiber.

Quick cooking tip: To store the stock, refrigerate it in covered 2-cup containers for up to 3 days, or freeze it for up to 3 months.

Chicken Stock

A fast-to-make stock with only 1 gram of fat.

Yields: about 9 cups

olive-oil nonstick spray

1 pound chicken breasts

2 celery stalks, leaves included, halved

4 large onions, with skins, quartered

4 medium carrots, halved

1 small turnip, quartered

2 bay leaves

8 whole black peppercorns

1 sprig parsley

1 sprig thyme

10 cups water

Coat a nonstick skillet with the spray and warm it over medium-high heat for 1 minute. Add the chicken and cook it until the pieces are browned on all sides. Transfer the chicken to an 8-quart pot. Add the celery, onions, carrots, turnips, bay leaves, peppercorns, parsley, thyme, and water. Cover the pot, and bring the mixture to a boil. Reduce the heat, and simmer for 1 hour.

Pour the stock through a large strainer into a large bowl or pot. Discard the chicken bones, vegetables, and seasonings; reserve the chicken breast meat for another use. Chill the stock, then skim and discard the fat that's accumulated on the top of the liquid.

Per cup: 40 calories, 1 g fat, 0 g saturated fat, 0 mg cholesterol, 68 mg sodium, 0 g dietary fiber.

Quick cooking tip: To store the stock, refrigerate it in covered 2-cup containers for up to 3 days, or freeze it for up to 3 months.

Turkey Stock

A great way to use up leftover turkey wings.

Yields: about 9 cups

2 roasted turkey wings, skin included

2 celery stalks, leaves included, halved

3 large onions, with skins, quartered

2 medium carrots, halved

1 small turnip, quartered

1 parsnip

2 bay leaves

8 whole black peppercorns

1 sprig parsley

1 sprig sage

10 cups water

Combine the turkey, celery, onions, carrots, turnips, parsnip, bay leaves, peppercorns, parsley, sage, and water in an 8-quart pot. Cover the pot, and bring the mixture to a boil. Reduce the heat, and simmer for 1 hour.

Pour the stock through a large strainer into a large bowl or pot. Discard the turkey, vegetables and seasonings. Chill the stock; then skim and discard the fat that's accumulated on the top of the liquid.

Per cup: 45 calories, 1 g fat, 0 g saturated fat, 0 mg cholesterol, 55 mg sodium, 0 g dietary fiber.

Quick cooking tip: To store the stock, refrigerate it in covered 2-cup containers for up to 3 days, or freeze it for up to 3 months.

Vegetable Stock

The tastiest vegetable stock I've ever tried, and it's exceptionally easy to make.

Yields: about 9 cups

   4 large onions, quartered

   4 medium carrots, halved

   4 celery stalks, leaves included, halved

   10 basil leaves

   2 bay leaves

   2 cloves garlic

   8 whole black peppercorns

   1 sprig parsley

   10 cups water

Combine the onions, carrots, celery, basil leaves, bay leaves, garlic, peppercorns, parsley, and water in an 8-quart pot. Cover the pot, and bring the mixture to a boil. Reduce the heat, and simmer for 25 minutes.

Pour the stock through a large strainer into a large bowl or pot. Discard the vegetables and seasonings.

Per cup: 43 calories, 0.2 g fat, 0 g saturated fat, 0 g cholesterol, 37 mg sodium, 0 g dietary fiber.

Quick cooking tip: To store the stock, refrigerate it in covered 2-cup containers for up to 3 days, or freeze it for up to 3 months.

Chunky Chowders

Butternut Chowder with Smoked Salmon

This soup is everything a chowder should be: thick, creamy, chunky, and flavorful!

Makes: 4 servings

- 1 pound butternut squash, peeled and cut into ½-inch cubes
- 1 can (14 ounces) reduced-sodium vegetable broth
- 1 large white onion, chopped
- ½ teaspoon dried rosemary
- ¼ teaspoon white pepper
- 1 can (15 ounces) cream-style corn
- 1 cup frozen corn
- 8 ounces smoked salmon bits
- ½ cup 2% milk

Combine the squash, broth, onions, rosemary and pepper in a 4-quart pot. Cover the pot, and bring the mixture to a boil. Reduce the heat, and simmer until the squash is tender, 12 to 15 minutes. Using a potato masher, mash the vegetables until the mixture is smooth.

Stir in the cream-style corn, the frozen corn and salmon. Cover and simmer 10 minutes more. Stir in the milk.

Per serving: 230 calories, 3.6 g fat, 1 g saturated fat, 15 mg cholesterol, 510 mg sodium, 10 g dietary fiber.

Quick cooking tip: For maximum rosemary flavor, crush the herb in your fingers before adding it to the chowder.

Chicken–Corn Chowder with Stuffed Olives

In this simple recipe, tasty go-togethers–chicken and corn–make for a family-favorite chowder. Mashed potatoes thicken the broth; garlic and hot-pepper sauce impart zing.

Makes: 4 servings

- 1 teaspoon olive oil
- ¾ pound chicken breast, cut into ½-inch cubes
- 1½ cups chicken broth
- 1 large potato, peeled and cut into ½-inch cubes
- 4 cloves garlic, crushed
- 1 can (15 ounces) reduced-sodium cream-style corn
- 1½ cups frozen corn
- 4 scallions, sliced
- ½ cup 2% milk
- 2 to 3 drops Louisiana hot-pepper sauce
- 1 tablespoon chopped stuffed olives

Warm the oil in a 4-quart pot over medium-high heat for 1 minute. Add the chicken and sauté until the pieces are cooked through and lightly browned, 5 to 10 minutes. Transfer to a bowl, and cover it with foil to keep the chicken warm.

Pour 1 cup broth into the same pot. Add the potatoes and garlic. Cover the pot, and bring the mixture to a boil. Reduce the heat, and simmer the mixture until the potatoes are tender, about 12 minutes. Using a potato masher, mash the potatoes.

Stir in the cream-style corn, frozen corn, scallions, milk, hot sauce, chicken, and remaining broth. Heat until hot throughout, about 6 minutes. Stir in the olives and serve immediately.

Per serving: 318 calories, 6.1 g fat, 1.6 g saturated fat, 75 mg cholesterol, 373 mg sodium, 6.1 g dietary fiber.

Quick cooking tip: Add hot-pepper sauce with caution, tasting the soup after each drop. Why? The firepower of hot-pepper sauces varies dramatically. Some are mild; others, scorching.

Chili Chicken Chowder

Here's a knockout chowder with signature Southwest flavors: cumin, garlic, and chili. And they play exceptionally well with the basics: chicken, beans, potatoes, carrots, and tomatoes.

Makes: 6 servings

½ pound cooked chicken breast, cubed

1 can (14 ounces) fat-free chicken broth

1 can (14 ounces) diced tomatoes

1 can (15 ounces) black beans, rinsed and drained

1 red potato, diced

1 large carrot, thinly sliced

2 cloves garlic, minced

½ teaspoon cumin seeds

2 teaspoons chili powder

Combine the chicken, broth, tomatoes, beans, potatoes, carrots, garlic, cumin seeds, and chili powder in a 4-quart pot. Cover the pot, and bring the mixture to a boil. Reduce the heat, and simmer until the potatoes and carrots are tender, 15 to 20 minutes.

Per serving: 305 calories, 3.4 g fat, 0.7 g saturated fat, 32 mg cholesterol, 137 mg sodium, 12.8 g dietary fiber.

Quick cooking tip: Use ground cumin, if you can't get the seeds.

Variation: You may substitute turkey for the chicken and pinto beans for the black beans.

Easy Manhattan-Style Clam Chowder

Tomato clam chowder aficionados: This chunky version is brimming with clams, tomatoes, potatoes, and bacon, and is ready to serve in less than 20 minutes.

Makes: 4 servings

4 ounces Canadian bacon, diced

1 large Spanish onion, chopped

1 stalk celery, thinly sliced

1 can (10 ounces) clam juice

1 can (15 ounces) whole tomatoes, cut up

2 medium red potatoes, chopped

2 bay leaves

¼ teaspoon lemon pepper

1 can (6 ounces) minced clams with juice

¼ cup snipped fresh parsley

Sauté the bacon in a 4-quart pot until lightly browned. Add the onions and celery, and sauté until the onions are transparent, about 3 minutes.

Stir in the clam juice, tomatoes, potatoes, bay leaves and lemon pepper. Cover the pot, and bring the mixture to a boil. Reduce the heat, and simmer until the potatoes are tender, 12 to 15 minutes.

Stir in the clams and simmer the soup for 5 minutes more. Discard the bay leaves. Top each serving with the parsley.

Per serving: 182 calories, 1.6 g fat, 0.7 g saturated fat, 17 mg cholesterol, 697 mg sodium, 4.8 g dietary fiber.

Quick cooking tip: If you use fresh minced clams, keep the cooking time short, 5 to 10 minutes, or the clams will be tough.

Flounder–Jack Chowder

Taste-testers pronounced this creamy seafood and cheese chowder delicious. I think you'll agree.

Makes: 4 servings

2 teaspoons butter

1 large onion, chopped

2 celery stalks, chopped

2 cloves garlic

2 large potatoes, peeled and cut into ½-inch cubes

1 can (14 ounces) fat-free chicken broth

1 pound flounder, cut into bite-size pieces

½ cup skim milk

½ cup shredded reduced-sodium Monterey Jack cheese

1 teaspoon Louisiana-style hot-pepper sauce

2 tablespoons snipped fresh chives

Melt butter in a 4-quart pot over medium-high heat. Add the onions, celery, and garlic, and cook them until the onions are golden, about 3 minutes. Add the potatoes and broth. Cover the pot, and bring the mixture to a boil. Reduce the heat, and simmer until the potatoes and celery are tender, about 12 minutes. Using a slotted spoon, transfer 2 cups of the vegetables to a bowl; cover the bowl with foil to keep them warm.

Using a hand-held immersion blender, puree the vegetables remaining in the pot. Add the flounder. Cover the pot, and gently simmer the mixture until the fish is tender, 3 to 5 minutes. Gently stir in the milk, Monterey Jack cheese, hot-pepper sauce, and reserved vegetables. Heat until the soup is hot throughout; do not boil. Top each serving with chives.

Per serving: 339 calories, 6.6 g fat, 3.5 g saturated fat, 93 mg cholesterol, 368 mg sodium, 3.5 g dietary fiber.

Quick cooking tip: Flounder is a delicate fish. To keep it from falling apart, simmer and stir the soup gently.

Nor'easter Clam Chowder

When cold winds blow, warm up with this robust New England style chowder. It holds its own against the elements of hunger, and it's chockablock with flavor from clams, potatoes, corn, and bacon.

Makes: 4 servings

3 slices (about 2 ounces) smoked bacon

1 medium chopped onion

2 cans (6½ ounces each) minced clams

1 can (11 ounces) clam juice

2 medium red potatoes, diced

¾ cup frozen corn

1½ cup low-fat (2%) milk

2 teaspoons Worcestershire sauce

¾ teaspoon dried savory leaves

Cook the bacon in a 3-quart saucepan until it is browned, about 5 minutes. Transfer the bacon to a paper-towel-lined plate to drain. Add the onions to the pan, and sauté until they're translucent, about 3 minutes.

Drain the clams, reserving the juice. Add the canned clam juice, the potatoes, and the reserved juice to the pan. Cook the mixture until the potatoes are tender, 15 to 20 minutes.

Using a slotted spoon, transfer half the mixture to a bowl; cover with foil to keep warm. Using a hand-held immersion blender, puree the onion mixture in the pan. Return the reserved vegetables to the pan, and stir in the corn, milk, Worcestershire sauce, savory, and clams.

Heat the chowder on low (do not boil) until it is hot–5 to 10 minutes–stirring occasionally. Crumble the bacon, and top each serving with it.

Per serving: 371 calories, 8.6 g fat, 2.9 g saturated fat, 83 mg cholesterol, 698 mg sodium, 3.4 g dietary fiber.

Quick cooking tip: For a thicker chowder, use less clam juice.

Puerto Principe Chicken Chowder

Fusion cuisine is hot and so is this Caribbean goodie, which sports Spanish and Cuban influences. Look to sofrito sauce, hot-pepper sauce, and sunflower seeds for mouth-watering sizzle.

Makes: 4 servings

1 teaspoon olive oil

¾ pound boneless, skinless chicken breasts, cut into ½-inch cubes

1 onion, chopped

1 can (14 ounce) fat-free chicken broth

1 can (15 ounces) pigeon peas, rinsed and drained

1 pound tomatoes, chopped

2 cups packed torn chard leaves

2 tablespoons sofrito sauce

1 teaspoon Louisiana hot-pepper sauce

¼ cup sunflower seeds, toasted

Warm the oil in a 4-quart pot over medium-high heat for 1 minute. Add the chicken, and sauté the pieces until they are lightly browned, about 5 minutes. Add the onions, and sauté until they are translucent, about 3 minutes.

Stir in the broth, peas, and tomatoes. Cover the pot, and bring the mixture to a boil. Reduce the heat, and simmer for 10 minutes. Stir in the chard and sofrito, and cook, uncovered, for 1 minute.

Stir in the hot-pepper sauce. Top each serving with the sunflower seeds.

Per serving: 423 calories, 10 g fat, 2.2 g saturated fat, 99 mg cholesterol, 281 mg sodium, 9.9 g dietary fiber.

Quick cooking tip: Pigeon peas come in either green or yellow, and can be found in the international section of many supermarkets.

Scrod Chowder with Broccoflower

A cross between broccoli and cauliflower, broccoflower gives this chowder a splash of neon green color and mild cauliflower flavor.

Makes: 4 servings

3 cups cubed peeled potatoes

1 large onion, chopped

1½ cups clam juice

2 bay leaves

2 ounces prosciutto, finely chopped

½ teaspoon freshly ground black pepper

2 cups broccoflower florets

1 pound scrod fillet, cut into ¾-inch pieces

1 cup 2% milk

Combine the potatoes, onions, clam juice, and bay leaves in a 4-quart pot. Cover the pot, and bring the mixture to a boil. Reduce the heat, and simmer the mixture until the potatoes are tender, about 15 minutes. Using a slotted spoon, transfer half the potatoes and onions, including the bay leaves, to a bowl; cover with foil to keep the vegetables warm.

Using a potato masher, mash the vegetables in the pot. Stir in the prosciutto, pepper, and reserved vegetables. Cover the pot, and bring the mixture to a simmer. Add the broccoflower and scrod. Cook, covered, until the broccoflower is tender and the scrod is cooked through, 5 to 10 minutes.

Stir in the milk and heat the chowder until it is hot throughout, 3 to 5 minutes. Discard the bay leaves.

Per serving: 274 calories, 3 g fat, 1.2 g saturated fat, 61 mg cholesterol, 487 mg sodium, 4.2 g dietary fiber.

Quick cooking tip: Fish is cooked through if the layers are opaque from top to bottom.

Swiss–Butter Bean Chowder

Here's a robust chowder that boasts of bacon, Swiss cheese and plenty of great-tasting vegetables: carrots, cauliflower, butter beans, mustard greens. Fennel seeds add wonderful aniselike flavor.

Makes: 4 servings

2 slices smoked bacon

1 large red onion, chopped

2 cans (14 ounces each) fat-free beef broth

2 cups small cauliflower florets

1 can (15 ounces) butter beans, rinsed and drained

2 carrots, shredded

2 teaspoons white wine vinegar

2 bay leaves

½ teaspoon fennel seeds

2 ounces reduced-sodium Swiss cheese, shredded

½ cup torn mustard greens

Sauté the bacon in a 4-quart pot until crisp, about 3 minutes. Transfer to a plate lined with paper towels to drain. Wipe most of the bacon fat from the pot. Add the onions, and sauté them until they are translucent, about 5 minutes.

Stir in the broth, cauliflower, beans, carrots, vinegar, bay leaves, and fennel seeds. Cover the pot, and bring the mixture to a boil. Reduce the heat, and simmer for 12 minutes. Discard the bay leaves. Stir in the cheese, and heat until it has melted.

Crumble the bacon. Top each serving with the mustard leaves and bacon.

Per serving: 263 calories, 4.7 g fat, 2.1 g saturated fat, 13 mg cholesterol, 314 mg sodium, 9.3 g dietary fiber.

Quick cooking tip: Don't be tempted to substitute white distilled vinegar for the white wine variety; the distilled variety tastes quite harsh.

Cool Classics

Chilled Guacamole Soup

Holy guacamole, this is a subtly delightful soup. Its flavors—creamy avocado and sour cream—are quiet and pleasing. Its color—pale green—is quiet and soothing. And it all comes together in the pulse of a blender.

Makes: 4 servings

- 2 cans (14 ounces each) fat-free chicken broth
- 1 Florida avocado, cut into ½-inch cubes
- 1 cup nonfat sour cream
- 1 medium onion, chopped
- 2 tablespoons lemon juice
- 2 cloves garlic, crushed
- ½ teaspoon chili powder
- 1 teaspoon paprika, for garnish

Combine the broth, avocado, sour cream, onions, lemon juice, garlic, and chili powder in a blender jar. Process until pureed. Chill for 45 minutes. Top each serving with the paprika.

Per serving: 187 calories, 6.9 g fat, 1.4 g saturated fat, 0 mg cholesterol, 219 mg sodium, 4.8 g dietary fiber.

Quick cooking tip: Is your supermarket fresh out of Florida avocados? Then substitute a California variety. Just be aware that ounce for ounce the California fruit has more than twice the fat of the Florida kind.

Cold Dilled Tomato Soup

Chill out. Dill out. And enjoy this creative, sure-to-please soup. It fea-
tures tomato juice, sour cream, and sassy seasonings: red pepper
flakes, onions, ginger, curry, and lemon peel.

Makes: 4 servings

   3 cups low-sodium tomato juice

   1 celery stalk, chopped

   1 medium onion, chopped

   ¼ teaspoon red pepper flakes

   ½ teaspoon curry powder

   ¼ teaspoon ginger

   1 teaspoon grated lemon peel

   1 cup nonfat sour cream

   2 tablespoons snipped fresh dill or chives

In a 3-quart pot, bring 1 cup tomato juice to a boil. Add the celery, onions, and pepper flakes, and simmer for 10 minutes. Remove from the heat. Stir in the curry, ginger, lemon peel, and remaining 2 cups tomato juice. Transfer the mixture to a blender and puree. Chill for 45 minutes.

Stir in the sour cream. Top each serving with the dill.

Per serving: 111 calories, 0.2 g fat, 0 g saturated fat, 0 mg cholesterol, 99 mg sodium, 2.6 g dietary fiber.

Cucumber–Parsley Soup

This summertime refresher is truly "cool as a cucumber." Fresh parsley and dill make it extraordinary.

Makes: 4 servings

- 2 teaspoons canola oil
- ½ cup chopped onion
- 2 cups fat-free chicken broth
- 2 cups diced cucumber
- 1 cup diced peeled potato
- 1 cup parsley leaves
- ½ teaspoon dry mustard
- ½ teaspoon freshly ground black pepper
- 1 cup 2% milk
- ¼ cup snipped fresh dill

Warm the oil in a 4-quart pot over medium-high heat for 1 minute. Add the onions and sauté until they are transparent. Stir in the broth, cucumbers, potatoes, parsley, and mustard. Cover the pot, and bring the mixture to a boil. Reduce the heat, and simmer until the potatoes are tender, about 15 minutes. Remove from the heat, and let cool for 10 minutes.

Transfer the mixture to a blender jar. Process until pureed, and stir in the black pepper. Chill for 1 hour. Stir in the milk and top each serving with the dill.

Per serving: 143 calories, 3.9 g fat, 1 g saturated fat, 4.6 mg cholesterol, 130 mg sodium, 2.8 g dietary fiber.

Quick cooking tip: Peel the cucumber only if it is waxed.

Colorful Strawberry Soup
with Kiwi

Create a stir with this creamy soup, which is plump with strawberries, peaches, and kiwifruit. It's sweet. It's fruity. It's pretty. It's a hit with the young and young-at-heart.

Makes: 4 servings

- 1 pint (about 12 ounces) strawberries, sliced
- ¼ cup white grape juice
- 2 tablespoons honey
- 2 cups vanilla low-fat yogurt
- 2 peaches, peeled and chopped
- 1 kiwifruit, peeled and thinly sliced
- 8 fresh mint leaves, for garnish

Set 1 cup strawberries aside. Combine the grape juice, honey and remaining strawberries in a microwave-safe bowl. Microwave on HIGH for 3 minutes; let cool for 10 minutes.

Transfer the strawberry–juice mixture to a blender and add the yogurt. Process until pureed. Transfer to a bowl, and chill the mixture for 45 minutes.

Stir the peaches and reserved strawberries into the soup. Top each serving with the kiwi and mint.

Per serving: 205 calories, 0.5 g fat, 0 g saturated fat, 0 mg cholesterol, 73 mg sodium, 3.5 g dietary fiber.

Quick cooking tip: For fresh-looking peaches, cut them right before stirring them into the soup.

Delicate Vichyssoise with Roasted Peppers

Never had vichyssoise (pronounced vee-she-SWAHZ)? It's a potato-and-leek soup that's traditionally served cold and topped with minced chives. Now is a great time to give it a try. This version is coolly sophisticated, ultra-light, and extra easy to make.

Makes: 6 servings

- 2 teaspoons butter
- 2 large leeks, white part only, chopped
- 2 large waxy potatoes, peeled and diced
- 1 can (14 ounces) fat-free chicken broth
- ¼ teaspoon white pepper
- ¼ teaspoon celery seeds
- 1 teaspoon white wine vinegar
- 2 cups 2% milk
- ¼ cup chopped roasted red peppers

Melt the butter in a 4-quart pot over medium-high heat. Add the leeks, and cook until they are translucent, about 5 minutes. Stir in the potatoes, broth, pepper, celery seeds, and vinegar. Cover the pot, and bring the mixture to a boil. Reduce the heat, and simmer for 15 minutes. Remove pot from heat; let the mixture cool, uncovered, for 2 minutes. Transfer the mixture to a blender jar. Process until pureed.

Pour the mixture into a large bowl, stir in the milk, and chill the soup thoroughly, about 1 hour. Top each serving with the peppers.

Per serving: 154 calories, 3.2 g fat, 1.9 g saturated fat, 10 mg cholesterol, 115 mg sodium, 2.3 g dietary fiber.

Quick cooking tip: Roasted peppers from a jar work very nicely in this soup. Just be sure to drain them.

Fast Gazpacho

Hailing from Spain, gazpacho is an intriguing chilled soup of tomatoes, cucumbers, and other summertime vegetables. This version, which gets its zest from garlic and dried chili, is ready in the whirl of a blender's blade.

Makes: 4 servings

- 2 cans (15 ounces each) diced tomatoes
- 1½ cups reduced-sodium tomato juice
- 1 medium cucumber, chopped
- 1 green sweet pepper, chopped
- 1 medium onion, chopped
- 1 mild dried chili pepper, seeded and chopped
- 4 cloves garlic, chopped
- 2 teaspoons red wine vinegar
- 2 teaspoons olive oil
- 2 cups croutons, for garnish

Combine the tomatoes, tomato juice, cucumber, sweet pepper, onions, chili peppers, garlic, vinegar, and olive oil in a blender. Process the mixture until the vegetables are partially pureed. Chill the soup until cold, 30 to 40 minutes. Top each serving with croutons.

Per serving: 173 calories, 4.2 g fat, 0.7 g saturated fat, 0 mg cholesterol, 136 mg sodium, 5.4 g dietary fiber.

Quick Cooking Tips

- Ancho peppers, which are dried poblano peppers, give this recipe just the right zip. If you can't find them, simply use ¼ to ½ of a minced seeded cayenne pepper.
- Peel the cucumber only if it is waxed.

Red, Blue, and White Soup

Refreshingly tart flavors. Smooth, creamy texture. Vibrant red, blue, and white colors. All make this soup of blueberries, raspberries, and lemon yogurt a dinner winner.

Makes: 4 servings

- 2 cups blueberries
- 2 tablespoons honey
- ½ cup white grape juice
- 1¼ cups buttermilk
- 1 cup red raspberries
- ½ cup vanilla low-fat yogurt
- 1 teaspoon grated lemon peel

Combine the blueberries, honey, and ¼ cup grape juice in a microwave-safe bowl. Microwave on HIGH for 3 minutes. Transfer the blueberry mixture to a blender, and add ¾ cup buttermilk. Puree the mixture, and transfer it to a medium-size bowl. Chill for 1 hour. Rinse out the blender jar.

Combine the raspberries and remaining ¼ cup grape juice in a microwave-safe bowl. Microwave on HIGH for 2 minutes. Transfer the raspberry mixture to a blender. Puree the mixture, and transfer it to a small bowl. Chill for 1 hour.

Whisk together the yogurt and lemon peel. Whisk the remaining ½ cup buttermilk into the blueberry mixture. Divide the mixture among 4 serving bowls. Swirl some of the raspberry puree into each bowl of soup. Top each serving with a dollop of yogurt.

Per serving: 165 calories, 1.1 g fat, 0.5 g saturated fat, 2.7 mg cholesterol, 104 mg sodium, 4.2 g dietary fiber.

Spiced Mixed Fruit Soup

Apple juice and spice and everything nice—pears, watermelon, grapes and nectarines—that's what this heavenly soup is made of.

Makes: 4 servings

- 2 cups apple juice
- 1 cinnamon stick
- 2 whole allspice
- 2 lemon tea bags
- 2 cups vanilla low-fat yogurt
- 1 Bartlett pear, cored and chopped
- 1 cup cubed watermelon
- 1 cup white grapes
- 1 cup red grapes
- 1 nectarine, pitted and chopped

Combine the apple juice, cinnamon, allspice, and tea bags in a 2-quart saucepan. Cover the pot, and bring the mixture to a boil. Reduce the heat, and simmer for 5 minutes. Discard the cinnamon, allspice, and tea. Chill for 30 minutes.

In a serving bowl, whisk together the yogurt and 1½ to 2 cups of the juice mixture. Determine how much juice mixture to use by the consistency of the soup. Stir in the pears, watermelon, white grapes, red grapes, and nectarines.

Per serving: 251 calories, 0.8 g fat, 0.1 g saturated fat, 0 mg cholesterol, 76 mg sodium, 2.8 g dietary fiber.

Quick Cooking Tips

- Use a slotted spoon to fish out the cinnamon, allspice, and tea bags.
- For bright, fresh-looking pears and nectarines, cut them right before serving. When exposed to air, the flesh of those fruits oxidizes and turns brown.

White Peach Soup

White peaches, with their strip of brilliant red flesh, give this slightly sweet soup a soft pink tint. Red plums and green mint provide flavorful, colorful accents. It's a wonderful dish to serve for a cool lunch or a dessert.

Makes: 4 servings

4 medium white peaches, peeled and pitted

2 cups vanilla low-fat yogurt

¼ teaspoon cinnamon

1 teaspoon honey

2 red plums, pitted and coarsely chopped

1 teaspoon snipped fresh mint or ¼ teaspoon dried mint leaves

Combine the peaches, yogurt, cinnamon, and honey in a food processor. Process the mixture until it is smooth, about 30 seconds. Transfer the mixture to a serving bowl. Stir in the plums, and chill the soup for 30 minutes. Top each serving with the mint.

Per serving: 203 calories, 0.5 g fat, 0 g saturated fat, 0 mg cholesterol, 70 mg sodium, 3 g dietary fiber.

Quick cooking tip: Can't find any white peaches? Then use the standard yellow variety; just be aware that the soup's color will be a soft peach, not pink.

Variation: You may subsitute nectarines for the peaches and another variety of plums for the red plums.

Full of Beans

Bean Lover's Soup

Cause a stir with this super mixed-bean soup. It's flavored with carrots, spinach, and ham, and makes for a substantial meal in a dish.

Makes: 8 servings

16 ounces bean soup mix (mixed beans)

2 cans (14 ounces each) fat-free beef broth

2 cups water

2 carrots, sliced

2 cups torn fresh spinach

2 ounces deli baked ham, cut into ¼-inch cubes

1 teaspoon tarragon leaves

½ teaspoon lemon pepper

paprika, for garnish

parsley sprigs, for garnish

Rinse the beans and sort through them to remove debris. Place the beans in an 8-quart pot and add 6 cups water. Cover the pot and bring the water to a boil. Simmer for 3 minutes and remove the pot from the heat. Let sit for 1 hour. Drain the beans and return them to the pot.

Add the broth, 2 cups water, carrots, spinach, ham, tarragon, and lemon pepper. Cover the pot, and bring the mixture to a boil. Reduce the heat, and simmer until the beans are tender, about 1¼ hours.

Transfer half the mixture to a bowl; cover the bowl to keep the mixture hot. Using a hand-held immersion blender, puree the mixture in the pot. Return the reserved mixture to the pot. Heat until the soup is hot throughout, about 5 minutes; do not boil. Top each serving with the paprika and parsley.

Per serving: 229 calories, 1.1 g fat, 0.2 g saturated fat, 3.9 mg cholesterol, 187 mg sodium, 18.6 g dietary fiber.

Quick cooking tip: If you'd prefer not to wait an hour for the beans to soak in hot water, soak them in *cold* water in the refrigerator overnight instead.

Black-Eyed Pea and Corn Soup

Here's a hearty, homey soup, and it's high in flavor and low in fat. Smoked bacon, roasted red peppers, garlic, thyme, and fresh parsley punch up flavor and color.

Makes: 4 servings

    4 slices smoked bacon
    2 cups fat-free chicken broth
    1 can (15 ounces) black-eyed peas, rinsed and drained
    1 can (14 ounces) cream-style corn
    1 cup chopped red onions
    4 cloves garlic
    1 teaspoon dried thyme
    1/4 teaspoon white pepper
    1 cup roasted red peppers
    1/4 cup snipped fresh parsley

Cook the bacon in a 3-quart saucepan over medium-high heat until browned. Transfer to a paper-towel-lined plate to drain.

Add the broth, black-eyed peas, corn, onions, garlic, thyme, and white pepper to the saucepan. Cover the pot, and bring the mixture to a boil. Reduce the heat, and simmer for 15 minutes to blend the flavors.

Stir in the roasted peppers, and heat the soup for 1 minute more. Crumble the bacon. Top each serving of soup with bacon and parsley.

Per serving: 214 calories, 3.8 g fat, 1.2 g saturated fat, 9 mg cholesterol, 270 mg sodium, 10.9 g dietary fiber.

Quick cooking tip: If you are out of red onion, use a sweet onion.

Chili Bean Soup with Summer Squash

Few dishes are faster, easier, or tastier than this chunky bean soup, which sports fresh tomatoes, squash, and cilantro. It's ready to eat in just 20 minutes.

Makes: 4 servings

- 2 cans (14 ounces each) fat-free beef broth
- 1 large onion, chopped
- 2 carrots, thinly sliced
- 1 medium yellow summer squash, halved and sliced
- 3 cups canned chili beans with liquid
- 2 cups fresh tomatoes, chopped
- ¼ teaspoon freshly ground black pepper
- 1 teaspoon dried cilantro

Combine the broth, onions, carrots, and squash in a 4-quart pot. Cover the pot, and bring the mixture to a boil. Reduce the heat, and simmer until the carrots are almost tender, about 10 minutes.

Stir in the chili beans, tomatoes, and pepper, and simmer the mixture for 5 minutes more. Stir in the cilantro.

Per serving: 168 calories, 1.3 g fat, 0.6 g saturated fat, 0 mg cholesterol, 466 mg sodium, 9.9 g dietary fiber.

Quick cooking tip: If the summer squash doesn't look up to par, use zucchini in this recipe instead.

Variation: You may substitute fat-free chicken broth for the beef broth and zucchini for the yellow summer squash.

Curried Bean Soup

Here I offer an elegant, creamy soup with a soft yellow color and subtle curry flavor. It's easy to make as well.

Makes: 4 servings

2 cans (14 ounces each) fat-free chicken broth

1 cup canned garbanzo beans, rinsed and drained

1 cup canned great northern beans, rinsed and drained

1 medium potato, peeled and diced

1 leek, white part only, sliced

1 celery stalk, sliced

2 cloves garlic, chopped

2 teaspoons white wine vinegar

½ teaspoon curry powder

1 cup 2% milk

½ cup shredded reduced-sodium cheddar cheese

½ cup snipped fresh parsley

Combine the broth, garbanzo beans, great northern beans, potatoes, leeks, celery, garlic, vinegar, and curry powder in a 4-quart pot. Cover the pot, and bring the mixture to a boil. Reduce the heat, and simmer for 15 minutes.

Remove from the heat. Using a hand-held immersion blender, puree the mixture. Stir in the milk and cheddar. Return the soup to the heat, and warm it until the cheddar has melted and the soup is hot throughout (do not boil), 3 to 5 minutes. Top each serving with parsley.

Per serving: 235 calories, 3.9 g fat, 1.6 g saturated fat, 9.6 g cholesterol, 387 mg sodium, 6.7 g dietary fiber.

Quick cooking tips

- If you don't have an immersion blender, let the soup cool just enough to pour it safely into a regular blender. Process the soup and return it to the pot.
- For a slightly more pronounced color, use yellow cheddar cheese.

Easy Cannellini Bean and Potato Soup

Hankering for a comforting, hearty soup that goes together in a flash? Satisfy your cravings with this simply seasoned soup of beans, carrots, and potatoes. Tasters enjoyed it, and I think it'll more than meet your expectations.

Makes: 4 servings

 2 cans (14 ounces each) fat-free beef broth

 1 can (15 ounces) cannellini beans, rinsed and drained

 1 large potato, peeled and diced

 1 large onion, chopped

 1 celery stalk, sliced

 1 carrot, diced

 2 bay leaves

 1 teaspoon red wine vinegar

 ½ teaspoon fennel seeds

 ¼ teaspoon freshly ground black pepper

 1 cup croutons, for garnish

 ¼ cup snipped fresh cilantro, for garnish

Combine the broth, beans, potatoes, onions, celery, carrots, bay leaves, vinegar, fennel, and black pepper in a 4-quart pot. Cover the pot, and bring the mixture to a boil. Reduce the heat, and simmer until the potatoes are tender, about 15 minutes. Discard the bay leaves.

Transfer about half the vegetables to a bowl. Using a hand-held immersion blender, puree the vegetables in the pot. Return the reserved vegetables to the pot. Serve the soup garnished with croutons and cilantro.

Per serving: 206 calories, 0.7 g fat, 0 mg saturated fat, 0 mg cholesterol, 157 mg sodium, 8.4 g dietary fiber.

Quick cooking tip: For directions on making croutons, see the quick cooking tip under French Onion Soup.

Fresh Swiss Chard and Snap Bean Soup

Heads up, garlic lovers: This soup is brazen, bold, and assertive with the wonderful flavors of garlic and Swiss chard.

Makes: 4 servings

- 4 slices bacon
- 2 cans (14 ounces each) fat-free beef broth
- 4 large (8 medium) cloves garlic, thinly sliced
- ½ pound fresh green beans, cut into 1-inch lengths
- 1 small zucchini, quartered and sliced
- 4 ounces Swiss chard leaves, torn, stems removed
- ¼ teaspoon white pepper
- 1 sprig thyme

Cook the bacon in a nonstick skillet over medium-high heat until crisp. Transfer the bacon to a paper-towel-lined plate to drain. Let the bacon cool; crumble it.

Pour the broth into a 4-quart pot. Stir in the garlic, beans, zucchini, chard, pepper and thyme. Cover the pot, and bring the mixture to a boil. Reduce the heat, and simmer until the vegetables are tender, about 20 minutes. Discard the thyme. Serve garnished with the bacon.

Per serving: 92 calories, 3.4 g fat, 1.2 g saturated fat, 5 mg cholesterol, 314 mg sodium, 3.1 g dietary fiber.

Quick cooking tip: The fastest way to cut fresh green beans into 1-inch pieces is to "snap" them. Or you can line up several, about half a dozen is good, on a cutting board and cut all six beans at once.

Garbanzo Bean Soup with Pepperoni

Pepperoni makes this differently delicious soup really sing and perks up the basics: potatoes, sweet peppers, and garbanzo beans (or chickpeas, as they're known in many cooking circles).

Makes: 6 servings

4 cups fat-free beef broth

1 large potato, chopped

2 celery stalks, sliced

4 teaspoons dried minced onion

1 teaspoon cumin seeds

½ teaspoon dried thyme

1 can (15 ounces) garbanzo beans, rinsed and drained

1 small yellow sweet pepper, chopped

2 tablespoons diced cooked pepperoni

Combine the broth, potatoes, celery, onions, cumin, and thyme in a 4-quart pot. Cover the pot, and bring the mixture to a boil. Reduce the heat, and simmer for 12 minutes. Stir in the beans, pepper, and pepperoni. Simmer for 8 minutes.

Per serving: 179 calories, 5.7 g fat, 1.7 saturated fat, 7 mg cholesterol, 597 mg sodium, 5 g dietary fiber.

Quick cooking tip: By cooking and dicing pepperoni, you can maximize its flavor while minimizing its fat.

Great Northern–Cauliflower Soup

Pureed beans and potatoes are the secret behind the low-fat "creamy" texture in this superb soup. For contrasting texture, serve the soup with crunchy croutons, crusty bread or crisp crackers.

Makes: 4 servings

- 1 can (14 ounces) fat-free chicken broth
- 1 can (14 ounces) great northern beans, rinsed and drained
- 1 potato, peeled and cut into ½-inch cubes
- ½ pound cauliflower, cut into small florets
- 1 teaspoon minced dried onions
- ¼ teaspoon celery seed
- ¼ teaspoon freshly ground black pepper
- 1 cup skim milk
- ½ cup shredded Monterey Jack cheese
- paprika, for garnish

Pour the broth into a 4-quart pot; add the beans, potatoes, cauliflower, onions, celery seed, and black pepper. Cover the pot and bring the mixture to a boil. Reduce the heat; and simmer the mixture until the vegetables are tender, about 12 minutes.

Using a slotted spoon, transfer half the vegetables to a bowl; keep them warm. With a hand-held immersion blender, puree the vegetables in the pot. Stir in the reserved vegetables, milk, and Monterey Jack.

Cover the pot and heat the soup over low until it is hot throughout, about 5 minutes. Serve garnished with the paprika.

Per serving: 276 calories, 3.3 g fat, 1.9 g saturated fat, 11 mg cholesterol, 231 mg sodium, 8.9 g dietary fiber.

Hearty Minestrone with Elbow Macaroni

Minestrone means "big soup" in Italian, and traditional versions over-flow with pasta, beans, and other robust vegetables. This easy version lives up to its namesake.

Makes: 4 servings

1 carrot, thinly sliced

1 celery stalk, sliced

1 cup cut green beans

⅔ cup sliced scallions

1 can (14 ounces) low-sodium vegetable broth

1 teaspoon Italian herb seasoning

1 can (16 ounces) stewed tomatoes

pinch of cayenne pepper

1 tablespoon red wine vinegar

½ cup elbow macaroni

½ cup snipped fresh parsley

Parmesan cheese, optional

Combine the carrots, celery, beans, scallions, broth, Italian herb seasoning, tomatoes, pepper, and vinegar in a 4-quart pot. Cover the pot, and bring the mixture to a boil. Reduce the heat, and simmer for 25 minutes.

Stir in the macaroni, and cook the mixture for 7 minutes more. Serve the soup topped with parsley and Parmesan, if desired.

Per serving: 124 calories, 0.4 g fat, 0.1 g saturated fat, 0 mg cholesterol, 308 mg sodium, 2.3 g dietary fiber.

Quick cooking tip: Planning to double this recipe and serve half another time? Then add the macaroni to half the soup at a time; pasta tends to oversoften when stored in a broth.

Lentil Soup with Prosciutto

Prosciutto and Provolone cheese provide the pizzazz that sets this singular soup apart.

Makes: 4 servings

1 cup lentils

2 cans (14 ounces each) fat-free beef broth

1 medium red potato, diced

1 medium onion, chopped

2 stalks celery, sliced

2 cloves garlic, crushed

2 ounces deli prosciutto, thinly sliced and chopped

1/4 teaspoon freshly ground black pepper

1 cup packed torn fresh spinach

1/3 cup reduced-sodium Provolone cheese, shredded

1/4 cup cilantro leaves

Fill a 4-quart pot with water. Add the lentils. Cover the pot, and bring the mixture to a boil. Reduce the heat, and simmer for 3 minutes. Remove from the heat and let sit for 30 to 60 minutes.

Drain the lentils, and return them to the pot. Stir in the broth, potatoes, onions, celery, garlic, prosciutto, and pepper. Cover the pot, and bring the mixture to a boil. Reduce the heat, and simmer until the lentils and potatoes are tender, 12 to 15 minutes.

Stir in the spinach and Provolone cheese. Top each serving with cilantro.

Per serving: 296 calories, 3.4 g fat, 1.6 g saturated fat, 15 mg cholesterol, 360 mg sodium, 17 g dietary fiber.

Quick cooking tip: Lentils don't have to be soaked before they're cooked. If you skip that step, simply increase the cooking time by 30 to 45 minutes.

Navy Bean Soup with Shallots

This super-satisfying soup is creamy and rich tasting—thanks to pureed navy beans, Madeira wine, and Romano cheese.

Makes: 4 servings

8 ounces navy beans

2 teaspoons olive oil

3 medium (about 6 ounces) shallots

1 carrot, diced

1 celery stalk, sliced

¼ cup Madeira wine

2¾ cups reduced-sodium vegetable broth

1 teaspoon dried rosemary

¼ cup grated Romano cheese

¼ cup snipped fresh parsley

Rinse and sort the beans. Place the beans and 3 cups water in a 4-quart pot. Cover the pot, and bring to a boil. Reduce the heat, and simmer for 3 minutes. Remove from the heat and let sit for 1 hour. Drain the beans and return them to the pot. Add 4 cups water. Cover the pot, and bring to a boil. Reduce the heat, and simmer until the beans are tender, about 1 hour. Drain.

Warm the oil in the same 4-quart pot over medium-high heat for 1 minute. Add the shallots, carrots, and celery, and cook until the vegetables are soft, about 6 minutes. Stir in the Madeira and ¾ cup broth, and cook 6 minutes over medium heat.

Stir in the beans, remaining 2 cups of broth, and rosemary. Cover the pot, and bring the mixture to a boil. Reduce the heat, and simmer for 5 minutes. Using a slotted spoon, transfer half the mixture to a bowl; cover to keep the vegetables warm. Using a hand-held immersion blender, puree the mixture in the pot. Stir in the reserved vegetables, Romano, and parsley. Heat until the soup is hot throughout, about 2 minutes.

Per serving: 289 calories, 4.6 g fat, 1.5 g saturated fat, 3.9 mg cholesterol, 176 mg sodium, 14.8 g dietary fiber.

Quick cooking tip: Too rushed to cook beans? Then use 3 cups rinsed and drained canned white beans instead.

Shell Soup with Roman Beans

When your taste buds call out for an earthy country-style soup, try this pasta-and-bean version. It's fast. It's easy. And it's richly flavored— with ham, anchovies and Provolone cheese.

Makes: 4 servings

2 cans (14 ounces each) fat-free beef broth

2 carrots, thinly sliced

1 small onion, chopped

1 can (15 ounces) Roman beans, rinsed and drained

4 ounces pasta shells

¼ pound reduced-sodium deli ham, diced

½ can (1 ounce) anchovies, drained and mashed

¼ teaspoon crushed red pepper flakes

½ cup grated reduced-sodium Provolone cheese

Combine broth, carrots, and onions in a 4-quart pot. Cover the pot, and bring the mixture to a boil. Reduce the heat, and simmer for 5 minutes. Add beans, shells, ham, anchovies, and pepper. Simmer the mixture for 14 minutes. Stir in the Provolone, and cook for 1 minute more.

Per serving: 236 calories, 4.4 g fat, 2.2 g saturated fat, 23 mg cholesterol, 646 mg sodium, 3 g dietary fiber.

Quick cooking tip: Having trouble finding Roman beans? Then look for cranberry beans; sometimes that's the way they're labeled.

Smoky Garbanzo and Tomato Soup

Lebanon bologna and Marsala wine pair up to give this extra-easy soup an intriguing smoky flavor. Better prepare an extra batch; dining companions are likely to want seconds.

Makes: 6 servings

2 cans (14 ounces each) fat-free chicken broth

2 potatoes, peeled and diced

1 can (14 ounces) garbanzo beans, rinsed and drained

1 can (14 ounces) diced tomatoes

4 cloves garlic, chopped

2 scallions, thinly sliced

2 ounces Lebanon bologna, chopped

¼ teaspoon freshly ground black pepper

¼ teaspoon ground celery seed

1 tablespoon Marsala wine

snipped parsley, for garnish

Combine the broth, potatoes, beans, tomatoes, garlic, scallions, bologna, pepper, celery seed, and wine. Cover the pot, and bring the mixture to a boil. Reduce the heat, and simmer until the potatoes are tender, about 20 minutes.

Serve the soup garnished with parsley.

Per serving: 184 calories, 1.9 g fat, 0.4 g saturated fat, 5 mg cholesterol, 458 mg sodium, 5.6 g dietary fiber.

Quick Cooking Tips

- For a slightly thicker soup, use a hand-held immersion blender to partially puree the vegetables and bologna.
- Feel free to make this soup ahead. It stores exceptionally well in your refrigerator for a day or two, its smoky flavors blending marvelously.

Split Pea Soup

Here's an updated and easy version of old-fashioned comfort food, and it's full to the brim with split peas, smoked ham, leeks, and carrots. What else has it got? Less than 2 grams of fat and lots of fiber.

Makes: 4 servings

    8 ounces green split peas
    2 cans (14 ounces each) fat-free beef broth
    1 cup water
    2 ounces cooked smoked ham, chopped
    1 cup chopped leeks, white parts only
    1 cup diced carrots
    2 bay leaves
    1/4 teaspoon lemon pepper
    1/2 teaspoon ground coriander
    2 tablespoons snipped fresh parsley

Pour 3 cups water into a 4-quart pot. Add the split peas. Cover the pot, and bring the mixture to a boil. Reduce the heat, and simmer for 3 minutes. Remove the pot from the heat and let the peas soak for 1 hour. Drain the peas and return them to the pot.

Stir in the broth, 1 cup water, ham, leeks, carrots, bay leaves, lemon pepper, and coriander. Cover the pot, and bring the mixture to a boil. Reduce the heat, and simmer until the peas are tender, 45 to 60 minutes. Discard the bay leaves. Transfer half the mixture to a bowl; cover it with foil to keep the vegetables warm.

Using a hand-held immersion blender, puree the mixture in the pot. Return the vegetables to the pot. Heat until the soup is hot throughout, about 3 minutes. Top each serving with parsley.

Per serving: 259 calories, 1.6 g fat, 0.4 g saturated fat, 8 mg cholesterol, 314 mg sodium, 15.8 mg dietary fiber.

Quick cooking tip: If you're rushed, you can skip soaking the split peas, but be aware that you may need to cook them a few minutes longer.

Two Bean and Corn Chili Soup

This extra-easy, all-vegetable soup has the intense flavors of a hearty chili. For some crunch, serve it with baked tortilla chips.

Makes: 8 servings

- 1 large onion, chopped
- 1 medium green sweet pepper, chopped
- 3 cloves garlic, minced
- 1½ cups corn
- 1 poblano pepper, minced
- 1 can (28 ounces) crushed tomatoes
- 1 can (14 ounces) fat-free beef broth
- 1 can (15 ounces) red kidney beans, rinsed and drained
- 1 can (16 ounces) black beans, rinsed and drained
- 2 tablespoons chili powder
- 1 teaspoon ground cumin
- ¼ teaspoon ground allspice

Cook onions, sweet pepper, and garlic in a 4-quart nonstick pot over medium heat until the onion is translucent, about 7 minutes.

Stir in the corn, poblano, tomatoes, broth, beans, chili powder, cumin, and allspice. Cover the pot, and bring the mixture to a boil. Reduce the heat, and simmer the soup for 20 minutes.

Per serving: 449 calories, 2.2 g fat, 0.4 g saturated fat, 0 mg cholesterol, 75 mg sodium, 20 g dietary fiber.

Quick cooking tip: Don't have a nonstick pot? Then coat the bottom of a regular pot with nonstick cooking spray before cooking the onions, peppers, and garlic.

Quick Fava Bean Soup

Buttery-tasting fava beans and fresh tomatoes steal the show in this robust shortcut soup.

Makes: 4 servings

- 1 teaspoon olive oil
- 1 medium onion, chopped
- 4 cloves garlic
- 1 can (14 ounces) fava beans, rinsed and drained
- 1 medium yellow summer squash, chopped
- 2¾ cups fat-free beef broth
- 2 cups diced plum tomatoes
- 4 ounces Canadian bacon, chopped
- 1 teaspoon Italian herb seasoning
- 1 teaspoon red wine vinegar

Warm the oil in a 4-quart pot for 1 minute over medium-high heat. Add onions and garlic, and sauté them until the onions are golden. Add the beans, squash, broth, tomatoes, bacon, herb seasoning and vinegar. Cover the pot, and bring the mixture to a boil. Reduce the heat and simmer until the squash is tender, about 15 minutes.

Per serving: 133 calories, 3.8 g fat, 0.9 g saturated fat, 14 mg cholesterol, 497 mg sodium, 3.6 g dietary fiber.

Zucchini–Cannellini Soup

It's amazing how much intriguing flavor just a smidgen of smoked Lebanon bologna can add to this soul-satisfying soup.

Makes: 4 servings

- 2 teaspoons olive oil
- 1 can (16 ounces) low-sodium cannellini beans, rinsed and drained
- 1 small zucchini, thinly sliced
- 4 scallions, sliced
- 2 cloves garlic, minced
- 1 cup fat-free beef broth
- 1 cup water
- 1 slice (1 ounce) smoked Lebanon bologna, chopped
- ¼ teaspoon white pepper
- ¼ teaspoon celery seeds
- snipped fresh parsley, for garnish

Warm the oil in a 3-quart saucepan over medium-high heat. Add the beans, zucchini, scallions, and garlic, and cook until the zucchini is translucent, 8 to 10 minutes.

Transfer half the vegetable mixture to a food processor and puree it. Return the mixture to the saucepan. Pour in the water and beef broth. Stir in the bologna, pepper and celery seeds. Cover the pot and bring the mixture to a boil. Reduce the heat, and simmer the soup for 15 minutes. Garnish each serving with parsley.

Per serving: 151 calories, 3.5 grams fat, 0.6 g saturated fat, 4 mg cholesterol, 126 mg sodium, 6.4 g dietary fiber.

Mostly Vegetables

Asparagus Soup

*Can a soup be light, creamy, elegant, easy, and brimming with aspara-
gus, the harbinger of spring, all at once? Absolutely. Check out this
beguiling dish to be sure.*

Makes: 6 servings

1 pound asparagus

2 teaspoons canola oil

1 medium Spanish onion, chopped

1 medium potato, cut into ½-inch cubes

3 cups low-sodium vegetable broth

¼ teaspoon white pepper

½ teaspoon ground savory

1 cup 2% milk

¼ cup snipped fresh parsley

Cut off the asparagus tips. Cut the stalks into ½-inch slices, discarding
the woody bases. Blanch the tips and stalks for 3 minutes; plunge
them into cold water and drain them. Reserve the tips.

Warm the oil in a 4-quart pot over medium-high heat for 1 minute. Add
onions and sauté until translucent. Stir in the potatoes, broth, asparagus
stalks, and pepper. Cover the pot, and bring the mixture to a boil.
Reduce heat, and simmer until potatoes and asparagus are tender, about
12 minutes. Using a hand-held immersion blender, puree the mixture.

Stir in the milk and savory. Heat until it is hot throughout (do not boil),
about 3 minutes. Top each serving with parsley and asparagus tips.

Per serving: 111 calories, 2.9 g fat, 0.7 g saturated fat, 3 mg cholesterol, 75 mg sodium, 2.1 g dietary fiber.

Quick cooking tip: The easiest way to remove an asparagus's woody
base is to snap it off. If the stalk is tough, remove the outer layer with
a vegetable peeler.

Broccoli Bisque

Cooking time is short, so this soup has plenty of bright and fresh broccoli color and flavor. Nonfat sour cream adds body without fat.

Makes: 4 servings

1 can (14 ounces) fat-free chicken broth

1 small potato, finely chopped

1 small onion, finely chopped

½ teaspoon reduced-sodium soy sauce

2 cups broccoli florets

½ cup nonfat sour cream

½ cup 1% milk

¼ teaspoon fennel seeds, toasted and crushed

In a 4-quart pot, combine the broth, potatoes, onions, and soy sauce. Cover the pot, and bring the mixture to a boil. Reduce the heat, and simmer until the potatoes are tender, about 10 minutes.

Add the broccoli, and simmer the mixture until the broccoli is tender, 5 to 7 minutes. Using a hand-held immersion blender, puree the mixture, adding the sour cream, milk, and fennel. Heat the soup until it's hot throughout; do not boil.

Per serving: 106 calories, 0.6 g fat, 0.2 g saturated fat, 1.2 mg cholesterol, 160 mg sodium, 2.4 g dietary fiber.

Quick cooking tip: To toast fennel seeds, place them in a small, nonstick skillet. Warm them over medium heat until lightly browned, 3 to 5 minutes, shaking the pan occasionally.

Carrot Soup with Madeira

In this tamed version of a fiery Indian soup, curry provides a bit of nip that is balanced by smooth and flavorful Madeira.

Makes: 4 servings

2 cans (15 ounces each) reduced-sodium vegetable broth

1 pound carrots, thinly sliced

1 pound potatoes, peeled and cut into ½-inch cubes

2 medium onions, chopped

1 teaspoon curry powder

½ teaspoon thyme

1 cup low-fat (1%) milk

½ cup Madeira

Combine the broth, carrots, potatoes, onions, curry, and thyme in a 4-quart pot. Cover the pot, and bring the mixture to a boil. Reduce the heat, and simmer until the potatoes and carrots are very tender, 15 to 20 minutes.

Using a hand-held immersion blender, puree the vegetables, stirring in the milk a little at a time. Stir in the Madeira. Warm the soup until it is hot throughout.

Per serving: 178 calories, 0.8 g fat, 0.3 g saturated fat, 1.6 mg cholesterol, 104 mg sodium, 4.4 g dietary fiber.

Quick cooking tip: A food processor will make short work of chopping the vegetables for this recipe.

Variation: You may substitute fat-free chicken broth for the vegetable broth and sherry for the Madeira.

Celery–Leek Chowder

Dressed up with ham and paprika, this creamy chowder gets a light cheese flavor from ricotta.

Makes: 6 servings

1 teaspoon olive oil

3 leeks, white part only, sliced

⅛ pound finely diced deli smoked ham

2 large potatoes, peeled and diced

3 cups fat-free beef broth

1 celery stalk, sliced

1 teaspoon white wine vinegar

½ teaspoon ground celery seeds

¼ teaspoon white pepper

1 cup nonfat ricotta cheese

paprika, for garnish

Warm the oil in a 4-quart pot over medium-high heat for 1 minute. Add the leeks and ham; cook until the leeks are wilted, 3 to 5 minutes.

Stir in the potatoes, broth, celery, vinegar, celery seeds, and pepper. Cover the pot, and bring the mixture to a boil. Reduce the heat, and simmer for 15 minutes. Stir in the ricotta. Serve garnished with the paprika.

Per serving: 168 calories, 1.9 g fat, 0.5 g saturated fat, 9 mg cholesterol, 309 mg sodium, 2.6 g dietary fiber.

Quick cooking tip: After stirring in the ricotta, take care not to let the soup boil.

Cheddar–Butternut Soup

Here's a refreshingly new way to serve butternut squash. A crisp green salad and warm garlic bread make for perfect companions to this soup.

Makes: 6 servings

2 cans (14 ounces each) fat-free chicken broth

1 butternut squash, cut into 1-inch cubes

2 potatoes, peeled and cut into ½-inch cubes

1 medium onion, chopped

3 cloves garlic, minced

¼ teaspoon freshly ground black pepper

¼ teaspoon ground nutmeg

1 cup shredded reduced-fat cheddar cheese

paprika, for garnish

Combine the broth, squash, potatoes, onions, garlic, pepper, and nutmeg in a 4-quart pot. Cover the pot, and bring the mixture to a boil. Reduce the heat, and simmer until the vegetables are tender, about 15 minutes.

Remove the pot from the heat. Using a potato masher, mash the squash and potatoes. Stir in the cheddar and serve garnished with the paprika.

Per serving: 170 calories, 2.2 g fat, 0.9 g saturated fat, 7 mg cholesterol, 135 mg sodium, 4.4 g dietary fiber.

Quick cooking tip: To save time, use 1 pound chopped butternut squash available in your supermarket's produce section.

Cheddar–Tomato Bisque

Here I've taken liberties with the definition of a bisque. This version has a beautiful burnt orange color, the special flavors of tomato and cheddar, and all the usual richness.

Makes: 6 servings

- 1 teaspoon olive oil
- 1 large onion, chopped
- 2 cans (14 ounces each) fat-free beef broth
- 2 large potatoes, peeled and cut into ½-inch cubes
- 4 plum tomatoes, chopped
- 1 carrot, shredded
- 2 cloves garlic, crushed
- ¼ teaspoon freshly ground black pepper
- ½ teaspoon ground dried savory
- 1 cup 2% milk
- ¾ cup shredded reduced-fat cheddar cheese
- ¼ cup snipped fresh parsley, for garnish

Warm the oil in a 4-quart pot over medium-high heat for 1 minute. Add the onions and sauté until they are translucent. Stir in the broth, potatoes, tomatoes, carrots, garlic, pepper, and savory. Cover the pot, and bring the mixture to a boil. Reduce the heat, and simmer until the vegetables are tender, about 15 minutes.

Remove from the heat and, using a hand-held immersion blender, puree the mixture. Stir in the milk and cheddar. Reheat until the soup is hot throughout (do not let it boil). Serve garnished with parsley.

Per serving: 177 calories, 3.5 g fat, 1.3 g saturated fat, 8 mg cholesterol, 150 mg sodium, 3.4 g dietary fiber.

Variation: You may subsitute fat-free chicken broth for the beef broth and sage for the savory. Eliminate the carrot and add ½ teaspoon sugar.

Chipotle–Sweet Potato Soup

The nippy chili- and cumin-laced flavors of the Southwest are among my favorites. Here, I've used both to create a captivating soup that you can throw together in 25 minutes or less.

Makes: 4 servings

2 cans (14 ounces each) fat-free beef broth

1 large sweet potato, peeled and shredded

1 carrot, shredded

1 medium onion, chopped

1 small chipotle pepper, seeded and chopped

½ teaspoon cumin seed

¼ teaspoon allspice

¼ teaspoon white pepper

½ cup reduced-fat Monterey Jack cheese

Combine the beef broth, sweet potato, carrots, onions, chipotle pepper, cumin, allspice, and white pepper in a 4-quart pot. Cover the pot, and bring the mixture to a boil. Reduce the heat, and simmer for 15 minutes.

Remove the pot from the heat; using a hand-held immersion blender, partially puree the mixture. Stir in the cheese until it melts.

Per serving: 160 calories, 1.9 g fat, 0.8 g saturated fat, 5 mg cholesterol, 203 mg sodium, 5.4 g dietary fiber.

Quick cooking tip: Chipotles are smoked, dried jalapeño peppers. If you have trouble finding them, substitute a dried cayenne pepper and ⅛ teaspoon mesquite smoke flavoring, which should be added at the end of cooking.

Chunky Cream of Tomato Soup with Tarragon

There are good tomato soups. And there are great tomato soups. This version, with its fresh tomatoes, onions, and tarragon, is among the best. Try it; I'm sure you'll agree.

Makes: 4 servings

- 3 pounds ripe tomatoes
- 1 teaspoon olive oil
- 1 large onion, chopped
- 1 can (14 ounces) fat-free beef broth
- 1 tablespoon no-salt-added tomato paste
- 1 tablespoon brown sugar
- ¼ teaspoon freshly ground black pepper
- 1 cup 2% milk
- 1 teaspoon tarragon leaves
- ½ cup snipped fresh basil leaves

Peel and seed the tomatoes, reserving the juice. Cut the tomatoes into small chunks.

Warm the oil in a 4-quart pot over medium-high heat for 1 minute. Add the onions and sauté until the onions are golden (do not brown), about 5 minutes. Add the broth, tomatoes, tomato paste, sugar, black pepper, and reserved tomato juice. Cover the pot, and bring the mixture to a boil. Reduce the heat, and simmer the mixture for 10 minutes.

Stir in the milk and tarragon. Heat the soup until it is hot throughout (do not boil), about 3 minutes. Top each serving with basil.

Per serving: 160 calories, 3.6 g fat, 1.1 g saturated fat, 5 mg cholesterol, 134 mg sodium, 5.1 g dietary fiber.

Quick Cooking Tips

To peel and seed tomatoes easily, follow these steps:

1. Blanch tomatoes in boiling water for 1 minute and immediately plunge them into icy-cold water. Slip off the skins.

2. Cut the tomatoes in half horizontally.

3. Squeeze the halves over a sieve, and discard the seeds.

To store leftover tomato paste, follow these steps:

1. Coat a small baking sheet with cooking spray.

2. Drop the paste by the tablespoonsful onto the sheet, and place the sheet in the freezer for an hour.

3. Wrap each frozen dollop of paste in waxed paper and place in a freezer bag. Return the paste to the freezer.

Classic Potato and Leek Soup

Seasoned with ham and celery, this popular soup makes for a perfect accompaniment to a special dinner or a speedy supper. It's light. It's easy. It's splendid.

Makes: 4 servings

- 1 teaspoon olive oil
- 3 leeks, white part only, sliced
- ¼ pound, finely diced lean deli ham
- 3 cups diced potatoes
- 2 cups fat-free chicken broth
- ½ teaspoon ground celery seeds
- 1 cup low-fat (1%) milk
- ¼ teaspoon freshly ground black pepper

Warm the oil in a 4-quart pot over medium-high heat for 1 minute. Add the leeks and ham; cook until the leeks are wilted, 3 to 5 minutes.

Stir in the potatoes, broth and celery seeds. Cover the pot, and bring the mixture to a boil. Reduce the heat, and simmer for 10 minutes. Stir in the milk and pepper. Cook (do not boil) until the potatoes are tender, 5 to 10 minutes.

Per serving: 246 calories, 3.8 g fat, 1.1 g saturated fat, 18 mg cholesterol, 515 mg sodium, 3.6 g dietary fiber.

Quick cooking tip: For a light, delicate flavor, take care not to brown the ham and leeks.

Cream of Cauliflower and Parsnip Soup

Thick, satisfying, subtly nutty-tasting, and oh so good. What more could you want from a simple soup that's ready to eat in no time flat?

Makes 4: servings

- 1 teaspoon olive oil
- 4 ounces mushrooms, cubed
- 2 shallots, sliced
- 2 large potatoes, peeled and cut into ½-inch cubes
- 2 cups cauliflower, broken into florets
- 1 cup thinly sliced parsnips
- 2 cups low-sodium vegetable broth
- ½ cup skim milk
- ½ teaspoon sage
- ⅛ teaspoon white pepper
- paprika, for garnish
- parsley sprigs, for garnish

Warm the oil in a 4-quart pot over medium-high heat for 1 minute. Add the mushrooms and shallots, and sauté them for 3 minutes.

Stir in the potatoes, cauliflower, parsnips, and broth. Cover the pot, and bring the mixture to a boil. Reduce the heat, and simmer until the vegetables are tender, about 10 minutes. Using a hand-held immersion blender, puree the mixture.

Stir in the milk, sage, and pepper. Warm the soup until it is hot throughout, about 5 minutes; do not boil. Garnish each serving with the paprika and parsley.

Per serving: 177 calories, 1.6 g fat, 0.3 g saturated fat, 0.6 mg cholesterol, 82 mg sodium, 5.3 g dietary fiber.

Quick cooking tip: When pureeing the potatoes and other vegetables, take care not to overwhip them; they may become gummy.

Cream of Potato and Cauliflower Soup

Cheddar cheese and cauliflower make for a delectable pairing, especially in an extra-easy soup like this one.

Makes: 4 servings

- 1 can (14 ounces) low-sodium vegetable broth
- 1 potato, peeled and cut into ½-inch cubes
- ½ pound cauliflower, cut into small florets
- 1 cup skim milk
- ½ cup shredded cheddar cheese
- ⅛ teaspoon white pepper
- nutmeg, for garnish

Pour the broth into a 4-quart pot; add the potatoes and cauliflower. Cover the pot and bring the mixture to a boil. Reduce the heat; simmer until the vegetables are tender, about 12 minutes.

Using a slotted spoon, transfer half the vegetables to a bowl; cover with foil to keep them warm. With a hand-held immersion blender, puree the vegetables in the pot. Stir in the milk, cheese, white pepper and reserved vegetables. Cover and heat over low heat until hot throughout, about 5 minutes. Garnish each serving with nutmeg.

Per serving: 147 calories, 4 g fat, 2.3 g saturated fat, 15 mg cholesterol, 148 mg sodium, 2.6 g dietary fiber.

Quick cooking tip: Take care not to boil the soup after adding the milk, or it might curdle.

Variation: You may substitute fat-free chicken broth for the vegetable broth and Monterey Jack cheese for the cheddar cheese.

Creamy Carrot and Potato Soup

This incredibly thick soup has a warm golden color and tons of flavor, thanks to carrots, onions, thyme, and Canadian bacon.

Makes: 4 servings

- 1 can (14 ounces) fat-free chicken broth
- 2 large potatoes, peeled and cut into ½-inch cubes
- 1 large carrot, sliced ½ inch thick
- ½ teaspoon thyme
- ⅛ teaspoon white pepper
- 1 onion, chopped
- 2 ounces Canadian bacon, diced
- 4 ounces nonfat ricotta cheese
- snipped fresh parsley, for garnish

Combine the broth, potatoes, carrots, thyme, and pepper in a 4-quart pot. Cover the pot, and bring the mixture to a boil. Reduce the heat, and simmer until the potatoes and carrots are tender, 18 to 22 minutes.

Meanwhile, in a nonstick skillet, cook the onions and bacon until the onions are translucent, about 5 minutes. Remove from heat.

Using a hand-held immersion blender, puree the potatoes and carrots, stirring in the ricotta. Mix in the bacon and onions. Garnish each serving with parsley.

Per serving: 180 calories, 1.6 g fat, 0.6 saturated fat, 11 mg cholesterol, 359 mg sodium, 3.3 g dietary fiber.

Quick cooking tip: For a thinner soup, add skim milk or additional chicken broth. Heat the soup until it is hot throughout.

French Onion Soup

In this quick version of the French classic, Madeira wine and Gruyère cheese impart wonderful mellow and nutty flavors. Crisp croutons soak up the tasty broth.

Makes: 4 servings

1 teaspoon olive oil

4 medium onions, cut into thin wedges

4 cans fat-free beef broth

1 tablespoon Madeira wine

3 cups plain croutons

½ cup shredded Gruyère cheese

½ cup snipped fresh parsley

Warm the oil in a 4-quart pot over medium-high heat for 1 minute. Add the onions, and sauté until they're golden, about 8 minutes. Add the broth. Cover the pot, and bring the mixture to a boil. Reduce the heat, and simmer for 15 minutes. Stir in the Madeira.

Divide the croutons and cheese among 4 soup bowls. Ladle in the soup, and top each serving with parsley.

Per serving: 249 calories, 7.4 g fat, 3.2 g saturated fat, 16 mg cholesterol, 477 mg sodium, 3.4 g dietary fiber.

Quick cooking tip: To make croutons, cut white or whole wheat bread into ¾-inch cubes. Spread the cubes on a baking sheet and mist them with cooking spray. Broil until they're golden, about 3 minutes. Shake the pan or stir the cubes to expose the untoasted sides. Mist with cooking oil spray and broil another 2 to 3 minutes.

Fresh Tomato–Corn Soup

In summer, when fresh vegetables and herbs are at their peak, create a sensation with this lively vegetarian soup. It comes together in a snap and takes less than 15 minutes to cook.

Makes: 4 servings

- 2 teaspoons olive oil
- 1 cup chopped red onion
- 4 cloves garlic, minced
- 1 can (14 ounces) low-sodium vegetable broth
- 2 cups diced zucchini
- 1 pound fresh tomatoes, chopped
- 1½ cups frozen corn
- ½ teaspoon crushed red pepper flakes
- ¼ cup snipped fresh basil leaves
- 2 tablespoons bacon bits, for garnish

Warm the oil in a 4-quart pot over medium-high heat for 1 minute. Add the onions and garlic, and sauté until the onions are translucent, about 3 minutes.

Stir in the broth, zucchini, tomatoes, corn, and red pepper flakes. Cover the pot, and bring the mixture to a boil. Reduce the heat, and simmer until the zucchini is tender, about 10 minutes.

Stir in the basil. Top each serving with the bacon bits.

Per serving: 151 calories, 3.9 g fat, 0.5 g saturated fat, 0 mg cholesterol, 136 mg sodium, 4.7 g dietary fiber.

Quick cooking tip: Keep the cooking time short so the tomatoes and zucchini retain their fresh flavors.

Hearty Parsnip–Turnip Soup

Because cooking time is short, the root veggies–parsnips, carrots, and turnips–in this soup taste flavorful yet mild. Dill and thyme provide just-right seasoning.

Makes: 4 servings

2 cans (14 ounces each) fat-free chicken broth

1 parsnip, diced

1 turnip, diced

1 yellow summer squash, diced

1 carrot, diced

1 potato, peeled and diced

1 onion, chopped

½ teaspoon thyme leaves

¼ teaspoon freshly ground black pepper

¼ teaspoon dill weed

¼ teaspoon paprika, for garnish

Combine the broth, parsnips, turnips, squash, carrots, potatoes, onions, thyme, pepper, and dill weed in a 4-quart pot. Cover the pot, and bring the mixture to a boil. Reduce the heat, and simmer until the vegetables are tender, about 12 minutes. Transfer half the vegetables to a bowl; cover with foil to keep them warm.

Using a hand-held immersion blender, puree the vegetables remaining in the pot. Return the reserved vegetables to the pot. Serve garnished with the paprika.

Per serving: 147 calories, 0.4 g fat, 0.1 g saturated fat, 0 mg cholesterol, 185 mg sodium, 6 g dietary fiber.

Jalapeño Jack Potato Soup

I just love the way cheese and ordinary potatoes create a yummy soup to die for! For crunch, serve this soup with crudités, croutons, or crusty French bread.

Makes: 4 servings

> 6 large or 10 medium potatoes, peeled and
> cut into ½-inch cubes
>
> 1 can (14 ounces) fat-free chicken broth
>
> 1 medium onion, finely chopped
>
> ½ teaspoon celery seeds
>
> 1 cup skim milk
>
> 1 cup shredded jalapeño Monterey Jack cheese
>
> caraway seeds, for garnish

Combine the potatoes, broth, onions, and celery seeds in a 4-quart pot. Cover the pot, and bring the mixture to a boil. Reduce the heat, and simmer until the potatoes are tender, 15 to 20 minutes.

Using a potato masher or hand-held immersion blender, mash the potatoes, stirring in the milk a little at a time. Mix in the cheese and cook until it has melted, about 5 minutes. Garnish each serving with the caraway seeds.

Per serving: 350 calories, 9.6 g fat, 6.2 g saturated fat, 32 mg cholesterol, 279 mg sodium, 4.6 g dietary fiber.

Quick cooking tip: To make this soup still lower in fat, you can use a fat-free cheese, such as fat-free cheddar or Swiss. Just be aware that the flavor and texture will be different.

Portobello Mushroom Soup

For mushroom aficionados, here's a splendid soup that's thick and dark with tons of substantial portobello mushrooms. For mellowness, I've added a splash of dry sherry, and for bright color, I've topped each serving with snipped chives.

Makes: 4 servings

> 2 teaspoons butter
>
> 6 ounces small portobello mushrooms, sliced
>
> 1 large onion, chopped
>
> 2 cups fat-free chicken broth
>
> 1 large potato, peeled and shredded
>
> 2 bay leaves
>
> 1/4 teaspoon white pepper
>
> 1 cup 2% milk
>
> 1 tablespoon dry sherry
>
> 1/4 cup snipped fresh chives

Reserve 4 attractive mushroom slices for a garnish.

Melt the butter in a 4-quart pot over medium-high heat. Add the mushrooms and onions, and sauté until the onions are translucent. Stir in the broth, potatoes, and bay leaves. Cover the pot, and bring the mixture to a boil. Reduce the heat, and simmer for 15 minutes. Discard the bay leaves. Stir in the pepper.

Using a hand-held immersion blender, puree the mixture. Stir in the milk and sherry. Heat the soup until it is hot throughout (do not boil), about 5 minutes. Top each serving with chives and the reserved mushroom slices.

Per serving: 156 calories, 3.6 g fat, 2 g saturated fat, 10 mg cholesterol, 143 mg sodium, 2.7 g dietary fiber.

Quick cooking tip: To clean mushrooms, wipe them with a damp paper towel or rinse them quickly under cool running water. Never soak mushrooms; their flavor will be diluted.

Potato–Marsala Soup with Herbes de Provence

This differently delicious soup gives a whole new meaning to fast food. Prosciutto adds panache while roasted red peppers lend color.

Makes: 4 servings

- 2½ cups fat-free chicken broth
- 3 cups diced peeled potatoes
- 1 large onion, chopped
- 1 celery stalk, chopped
- ½ cup Marsala wine
- 2 ounces prosciutto, chopped
- ½ teaspoon herbes de Provence
- ¼ cup diced roasted red peppers

Combine the broth, potatoes, onions, celery, wine, prosciutto, and herbes in a 4-quart pot. Cover the pot, and bring the mixture to a boil. Reduce the heat, and simmer until the potatoes are tender, 12 to 15 minutes.

Using a hand-held immersion blender, process the mixture until it is partially pureed. Top each serving with the roasted peppers.

Per serving: 207 calories, 1.5 g fat, 0.5 g saturated fat, 8.2 mg cholesterol, 262 mg sodium, 3.5 g dietary fiber.

Quick cooking tip: Herbes de Provence is a commercial blend of dried herbs that's typical of the cuisine of southern France. If you can't find it in your supermarket, substitute a pinch each of rosemary, marjoram, thyme, and sage.

Shallot–Watercress Soup

Six ingredients–that's all it takes to make this sensational soup, which showcases piquant shallots and watercress. In each spoonful, a caper or two provides an intriguing burst of flavor.

Makes: 4 servings

- 2 teaspoons butter
- 8 shallots, thinly sliced
- 1 medium potato, finely chopped
- 2 cans (14 ounces each) fat-free chicken broth
- ½ bunch (about 2 ounces) watercress, leaves only
- 2 teaspoons capers, rinsed and drained

Melt the butter in a 4-quart pot over medium-high heat. Add the shallots, and cook them until they are translucent, about 3 minutes. Add the potatoes and ¾ cup broth, and cook until the potatoes are tender, about 10 minutes.

Using a hand-held immersion blender, puree the mixture. Stir in the remaining broth, and heat the soup until it is hot throughout, 3 to 5 minutes. Stir in the watercress, and heat for 1 minute more. Add the capers and serve immediately.

Per serving: 122 calories, 2.2 g fat, 1.3 g saturated fat, 5.5 mg cholesterol, 228 mg sodium, 1 g dietary fiber.

Simple Garlic Soup

Don't be intimidated by the amount of garlic in this recipe. Gentle cooking tames garlic's flavor and makes it mild, almost sweet.

Makes: 4 servings

- 1 teaspoon olive oil
- 1 head garlic, cloves peeled and sliced
- 2 cans (14 ounces each) fat-free chicken broth
- 1 tablespoon snipped fresh fennel leaves
- 1 tablespoon dry sherry
- 2 cups whole wheat bread croutons
- ¼ cup snipped fresh parsley

Warm the oil in a 4-quart pot over medium-high heat for 1 minute. Add the garlic, and sauté until golden (do not brown), 3 to 5 minutes, stirring constantly. Add the broth and fennel; simmer the mixture for 15 minutes. Stir in the sherry.

Top each serving with croutons and parsley.

Per serving: 150 calories, 2.3 g fat, 0.4 g saturated fat, 0 mg cholesterol, 252 mg sodium, 1.5 g dietary fiber.

Quick cooking tip: See the quick cooking tip under French Onion Soup for directions on making croutons.

Speedy Cheese Tortellini Soup

Need dinner on the double? Then you've opened to the right recipe. This easy soup takes just 10 minutes to cook, and it's packed with tomatoes, cheese tortellini, sweet peppers, and scallions.

Makes: 6 servings

2 cups coarsely chopped tomatoes

2 cans (14 ounces each) fat-free chicken broth

½ cup sliced scallions (about 3)

½ cup chopped red or green sweet peppers

1 teaspoon Italian herb seasoning

⅛ teaspoon celery seeds

¼ teaspoon crushed red pepper flakes

2 cups (about 1 pound) frozen tricolor cheese tortellini

1 tablespoon snipped fresh basil

Combine the tomatoes, broth, scallions, peppers, herb seasoning, celery seeds, and pepper flakes in a 4-quart pot. Cover the pot, and bring the mixture to a boil. Stir in the tortellini, and simmer the soup until the tortellini are al dente, about 10 minutes. Stir in the basil, and serve immediately.

Per serving: 123 calories, 2.3 g fat, 0.9 g saturated fat, 6.7 mg cholesterol, 234 mg sodium, 2.6 g dietary fiber.

Quick cooking tip: Because tortellini become soggy when stored in broth, serve this soup freshly made.

Variation: You may substitute fat-free beef broth for the chicken broth and sausage tortellini for the cheese variety. Small ravioli may be used instead of the tortellini.

Swiss–Potato Soup

A rich-tasting soup like this one needn't be reserved for special occasions. Why? It's rich in cheese flavor, not calories and fat, and it's ready to eat in 30 minutes or less.

Makes: 4 servings

1 teaspoon olive oil

1 large onion, chopped

1 can (14 ounces) fat-free chicken broth

2 large potatoes, peeled and cut into ½-inch cubes

1 celery stalk, chopped

⅛ teaspoon white pepper

½ teaspoon dried thyme leaves

1 cup skim milk

¾ cup shredded reduced-fat Swiss cheese

¼ cup snipped fresh chives, for garnish

Warm the oil in a 4-quart pot over medium-high heat for 1 minute. Add the onions and sauté until they are translucent. Stir in the broth, potatoes, celery, pepper, and thyme. Cover the pot, and bring the mixture to a boil. Reduce the heat, and simmer until the potatoes are tender, about 10 minutes.

Remove from the heat, and mash the mixture with a potato masher. Stir in the milk, and return the mixture to the heat. Stir in the cheese; cook until it melts, stirring constantly. Serve garnished with chives.

Per serving: 216 calories, 6.7 g fat, 3.9 g saturated fat, 15 mg cholesterol, 141 mg sodium, 2.8 g dietary fiber.

Quick cooking tip: If you can't find fresh chives, use the frozen or dried variety.

Tomato and Leek Soup

Here's a marvelous tomato soup that's way low in calories and fat. Beef broth and a measure of sherry are the secret flavor ingredients.

Makes: 8 servings

- 1 teaspoon olive oil
- 2 large leeks, white part only, thinly sliced
- 2 celery stalks, thinly sliced
- 2 cans (14 ounce each) fat-free beef broth
- 1 can (28 ounces) whole plum tomatoes, cut up
- 1 tablespoon brown sugar
- ¼ teaspoon lemon pepper
- 2 tablespoons dry sherry
- 2 bay leaves
- 2 teaspoons dried dill weed

Warm the oil in a 4-quart pot over medium-high heat for 1 minute. Add the leeks and celery, and sauté until the leeks are translucent and the celery is tender, about 5 minutes. Stir in the broth, tomatoes, sugar, pepper, sherry, and bay leaves.

Cover the pot and bring the mixture to a boil. Reduce the heat, and simmer the soup for 30 minutes. Discard the bay leaves. Stir in the dill.

Per serving: 73 calories, 0.7 g fat, 0.1 g saturated fat, 0 mg cholesterol, 294 mg sodium, 1.7 g dietary fiber.

Quick Cooking Tips

- Have some fresh dill on hand? (Maybe it'll bring good luck; the Ancient Romans thought it would.) Garnish each serving with a small sprig–along with a slice of lemon.
- For a vegetarian soup, substitute vegetable broth for the beef variety.
- Prefer a silky smooth tomato soup? After discarding the bay leaves, puree the soup, in batches, in a blender.

Zucchini Soup Margherita

Refreshing and light, this soup, which is brimming with mozzarella and basil, takes its name from a pizza specialty of Naples, Italy. According to legend, the cheese pizza was created to honor a Queen—Margherita.

Makes: 4 servings

2 teaspoons olive oil

8 ounces small zucchini, halved and sliced

1 medium onion, chopped

4 cloves garlic, chopped

2 cans (14 ounces each) fat-free chicken broth

8 ounces plum tomatoes, sliced

¼ teaspoon freshly ground black pepper

1 teaspoon balsamic vinegar

½ cup shredded part-skim mozzarella cheese, for garnish

½ cup snipped fresh basil, for garnish

Warm the oil in a 4-quart pot over medium-high heat for 1 minute. Add the zucchini, onions, and garlic, and sauté until the vegetables start to brown, 3 to 5 minutes. Stir in the broth, tomatoes, pepper, and vinegar.

Cover the pot, and bring the mixture to a boil. Reduce the heat, and simmer for 10 minutes. Serve garnished with the mozzarella and basil.

Per serving: 90 calories, 2.6 g fat, 0.4 g saturated fat, 0 mg cholesterol, 155 mg sodium, 2.2 g dietary fiber.

Catch of the Day

Crab Bisque

This delightful soup is elegant enough for a special dinner, easy enough for a casual supper, and fast enough to prepare anytime you wish.

Makes: 4 servings

butter-flavored cooking spray

1 medium onion, minced

1 can (10 ounces) clam juice

1 carrot, finely chopped

1 large potato, peeled and finely chopped

1 can (6¾ ounces) flaked crab meat

4 tablespoons fat-free cream cheese

⅛ teaspoon mace

1½ cups 2% milk

1 tablespoon sherry

¼ teaspoon paprika

⅛ teaspoon white pepper

Coat the bottom of a 3-quart saucepan with cooking spray. Add onions and cook over medium-high heat until translucent, about 3 minutes.

Stir in the clam juice, carrots, and potatoes. Cover the pan and simmer the mixture until the vegetables are tender, about 10 minutes. Stir in the crab meat, cream cheese, and mace. Using a hand-held immersion blender, puree the mixture until smooth.

Stir in the milk, and heat over low heat until the mixture is hot, 5 to 10 minutes. Stir in the sherry, paprika, and pepper; serve immediately.

Per serving: 168 calories, 2.4 g fat, 1.2 g saturated fat, 30 mg cholesterol, 524 mg sodium, 2.1 g dietary fiber.

Quick cooking tip: Cutting the potato and carrot into very small pieces, or even coarsely shredding them, will speed cooking.

Elegant Crab Soup with Madeira

I love crab meat. Here, my favored crustacean is featured with pota-
toes, cream cheese, and Madeira in a sophisticated, creamy soup
that's at home anytime—at a relaxed Sunday supper, a formal dinner
party, or a rushed weekday dinner.

Makes: 4 servings

1 teaspoon olive oil

1 medium onion, finely chopped

1 celery stalk, chopped

1 can (14 ounces) fat-free chicken broth

1 large potato, shredded

⅛ teaspoon white pepper

1 bay leaf

4 tablespoons fat-free cream cheese

1 can (10 ounces) flaked crab meat

1½ cups 2% milk

1 tablespoon Madeira

Warm the oil in a 4-quart pot over medium-high heat for 1 minute.
Add the onions and celery, and sauté until the onion is translucent.
Stir in the broth, potatoes, white pepper, and bay leaf. Cover the pot,
and bring the mixture to a boil. Reduce the heat, and simmer the mixture for 10 minutes. Discard the bay leaf.

Stir in the cream cheese. Using a hand-held immersion blender, puree
the mixture. Stir in the crab meat.

Stir in the milk, and heat the soup (do not let it boil) until it is hot
throughout. Stir in the Madeira. Serve immediately.

Per serving: 212 calories, 4.9 g fat, 1.7 g saturated fat, 79 mg cholesterol, 564 mg sodium, 1.5 g dietary fiber.

Quick Cooking Tips

• If you have a food processor, use it to shred the potatoes.

• Before stirring the crab meat into the soup, check it for bits of shell.

Orange Roughy and Carrot Soup

In this enticing soup, a hint of orange makes for a perfect complement to orange roughy. Pureed carrots and diced red pepper complete the flavor balance while giving the dish its eye-appealing color.

Makes: 6 servings

2 slices turkey bacon

1 large onion, chopped

3 cups clam juice

2 carrots, chopped

2 large potatoes, cut into ½-inch cubes

1 red sweet pepper, chopped

2 teaspoons grated orange peel

½ teaspoon lemon pepper

1 pound orange roughy, cut into bite-size pieces

1 cup 2% milk

Cook the bacon in a 4-quart pot over medium-high heat until browned and crisp. Transfer it to a paper-towel-lined plate to drain.

Add the onions to the pot, and sauté until they are translucent, about 5 minutes.

Stir in the clam juice, carrots, and potatoes. Cover the pot, and bring the mixture to a boil. Reduce the heat, and simmer the mixture until the potatoes are tender, about 12 minutes.

Using a potato masher, mash the mixture. Bring the mixture to a simmer, and stir in the sweet pepper, orange peel, and lemon pepper. Add the orange roughy, and cook, covered, until it is done, 3 to 5 minutes.

Stir in the milk, and heat until the soup is hot throughout, about 2 minutes. Crumble the bacon, and top each serving with it.

Per serving: 181 calories, 2.4 g fat, 0.7 g saturated fat, 22 mg cholesterol, 452 mg sodium, 3.1 g dietary fiber.

Quick cooking tip: For best flavor, use orange roughy within a day of purchase. In the U.S., it is imported frozen and deteriorates quickly after being thawed.

Provençale Bourride

This quick version of bourride, a Mediterranean seafood soup similar to bouillabaisse, nets unforgettable flavor from garlic, orange peel, and mayonnaise.

Makes: 4 servings

- 1 can (11 ounces) clam juice
- 2 cups dry white wine
- 1 cup chopped onions
- 1 cup sliced carrots
- 4 teaspoons minced garlic
- ¼ teaspoon freshly ground black pepper
- ¾ pound flounder, cut into bite-size pieces
- ½ teaspoon orange peel
- ½ cup fat-free mayonnaise
- 4 slices French bread, toasted

Combine the clam juice, wine, onions, carrots, garlic, and pepper in a 4-quart pot. Cover the pot, and bring the mixture to a boil. Reduce the heat, and simmer until the carrots are tender, about 15 minutes.

Add the flounder and orange peel, and simmer for 10 minutes more. Stir in the mayonnaise. Serve with the bread.

Per serving: 303 calories, 2.2 g fat, 0.5 g saturated fat, 58 mg cholesterol, 661 mg sodium, 2.5 g dietary fiber.

Sherried Scallop Soup
with Havarti

Here's a rich restaurant-style soup that's easy enough to make at home and fast enough to prepare on week nights. I'm sure you'll agree that the blend of scallops, cream sherry, and Havarti cheese is magnificent.

Makes: 4 servings

- 2 cans (11 ounces each) clam juice
- ½ cup water
- 2 potatoes, peeled and cut into ½-inch cubes
- 1 medium onion, chopped
- 2 bay leaves
- ½ cup cream sherry
- ½ cup shredded creamy Havarti cheese
- 1 pound bay scallops
- ½ cup 2% milk
- ¼ cup snipped fresh chives

Combine the clam juice, water, potatoes, onions, and bay leaves in a 4-quart pot. Cover the pot, and bring the mixture to a boil. Reduce the heat, and simmer until the potatoes are tender, 10 to 15 minutes. Discard the bay leaves.

Using a slotted spoon, transfer half the vegetables to a bowl; cover the bowl with foil to keep them warm. Add the sherry and Havarti to the pot. Using a hand-held immersion blender, puree the mixture in the pot. Return the reserved vegetables to the pot.

Stir in the scallops. Cover the pot, and simmer the soup until the scallops are cooked through, 5 to 10 minutes. Stir in the milk and heat until the soup is hot throughout, about 3 minutes. Top each serving with chives.

Per serving: 330 calories, 7.4 g fat, 0.4 g saturated fat, 66 mg cholesterol, 645 mg sodium, 2.9 g dietary fiber.

Quick cooking tip: After adding the sherry, cheese, and milk, do not let the soup boil, because it may curdle.

Shark Soup with Okra

Next time you grill up a flavorful shark steak, save a piece for this soup—it's different and delicious.

Makes: 4 servings

- 2 cans (14 ounces each) fat-free chicken broth
- 2 medium potatoes, peeled and cut into 1/2-inch cubes
- 1 large onion, chopped
- 2 teaspoons reduced-sodium soy sauce
- 1/4 teaspoon freshly ground black pepper
- 1/4 pound black tip shark steak, cooked and cut into 1/2-inch cubes
- 8 ounces whole fresh (or frozen and thawed) okra, sliced 1/2-inch thick
- 1/2 cup frozen peas
- snipped fresh parsley, for garnish

Combine the broth, potatoes, onions, soy sauce, and pepper in a 4-quart pot. Cover the pot, and bring the mixture to a boil. Reduce the heat, and simmer for 12 minutes.

Stir in the shark, okra, and peas. Cover and simmer 6 minutes more. Serve garnished with parsley.

Per serving: 192 calories, 1.6 g fat, 0.3 g saturated fat, 15 mg cholesterol, 289 mg sodium, 5.1 g dietary fiber.

Quick cooking tip: When slicing okra, discard the stem ends.

Shrimp–Rice Soup

A generous splash of lime gives this simple soup a refreshing flavor twist.

Makes: 4 servings

2 cans (14 ounces each) fat-free chicken broth

1 small onion, finely chopped

1 celery stalk, thinly sliced

¼ cup brown rice

½ pound medium shrimp, shelled, deveined, and cut into thirds

⅛ teaspoon crushed red pepper flakes

1 tablespoon lime peel

juice of 1 lime

Pour the chicken broth into a 4-quart pot, add the onions, celery, and brown rice. Cover the pot, and bring the mixture to a boil. Reduce the heat, and simmer until the rice is tender, about 40 minutes.

Stir in the shrimp and simmer until they are pink and cooked through, about 5 minutes. Stir in the pepper flakes, lime peel, and lime juice.

Per serving: 142 calories, 1.4 g fat, 0.3 g saturated fat, 86 mg cholesterol, 235 mg sodium, 1.2 g dietary fiber.

Quick Cooking Tips

- Supermarket running a sale on salad shrimp? (Those are the itty-bitty ones in which about 100 equal a pound; by contrast, there are about 35 medium shrimp in a pound.) If you want, you can switch to the miniatures in this recipe; just don't cut them into thirds.

- No time for shelling and deveining shrimp? Then pick up cleaned and cooked shrimp at the market, and cut the final cooking time to 3 minutes.

Szechuan Shrimp with Cellophane Noodles

Got a yen for a slightly spicy soup? Here's an attractive version to try. It has shrimp, bamboo shoots, scallions, red sweet pepper, and cellophane noodles. Chinese chili sauce and five-spice powder give it just-right Chinese character and zest.

Makes: 4 servings

4 ounces cellophane noodles, broken into short lengths

2 cans (14 ounces each) reduced-sodium vegetable broth

¼ cup rice wine vinegar

2 tablespoons Chinese chili sauce with garlic

½ pound large shrimp, peeled and deveined

½ can (4 ounces) sliced bamboo shoots, drained

1 cup sliced scallions

¼ teaspoon Chinese five-spice powder

1 red sweet pepper, cut into thin rings

Fill a 3-quart saucepan with water. Warm it over medium-high heat until hot but not boiling. Add the noodles; soak them for 10 minutes; drain.

Combine the broth, vinegar, and chili sauce in a 4-quart pot. Cover the pot, and bring the mixture to a boil. Add the shrimp, reduce the heat, and simmer until the shrimp is almost done, 2 to 3 minutes.

Stir in the bamboo shoots, scallions, peppers, and five-spice powder. Simmer the mixture for 5 minutes. Stir in the noodles. Simmer the soup for 3 minutes.

Per serving: 220 calories, 0.8 g fat, 0.2 g saturated fat, 87 mg cholesterol, 184 mg sodium, 1.8 g dietary fiber.

Quick cooking tip: If you can't find cellophane noodles, substitute bean threads or rice sticks.

Teriyaki, Snowpea, and Scallop Soup

Here's a light and delightful Asian-style soup with an unforgettable balance of complex flavors—snow peas and scallops seasoned with gingerroot, garlic, teriyaki sauce, and Marsala.

Makes: 4 servings

- 2 cups water
- 2 cups vegetable broth
- 1 tablespoon grated gingerroot
- 4 cloves garlic, crushed
- 1 teaspoon peanut oil
- 2 teaspoons teriyaki sauce
- 1 tablespoon Marsala wine
- 1/4 pound snow peas
- 1 pound bay scallops
- 2 scallions, sliced
- 1/4 teaspoon lemon pepper

Combine the water, broth, gingerroot, and garlic in a 4-quart pot. Cover the pot, and bring the mixture to a boil. Reduce the heat, and simmer for 15 minutes.

Stir in the oil, teriyaki sauce, and Marsala. Cover the pot, and return the mixture to a boil. Add the snow peas, and cook for 1 minute. Stir in the scallops, scallions, and lemon pepper, and simmer until the peas are crisp-tender and the scallops are done, about 3 minutes.

Per serving: 157 calories, 2.1 g fat, 0.3 g saturated fat, 37 mg cholesterol, 415 mg sodium, 1 g dietary fiber.

Quick cooking tip: Take care not to overcook scallops or they will become tough and rubbery. Scallops are done when they are opaque from top to bottom.

Poultry Plus

Chicken–Ditalini Soup with Cannelini Beans

Here's a change-of-pace chicken soup. It uses ditalini instead of the usual noodles and adds beans for extra fiber and flavor.

Makes: 4 servings

- 1 teaspoon olive oil
- ½ pound boneless, skinless chicken breast, cut into ½-inch cubes
- ¼ teaspoon freshly ground black pepper
- 4 cloves garlic, chopped
- 1 shallot, chopped
- 2 cans (16 ounces each) fat-free chicken broth
- 1 can (15 ounces) cannelini beans, rinsed and drained
- 2 carrots, thinly sliced
- 1 celery stalk, thinly sliced
- 2 bay leaves
- 1 sprig fresh lemon thyme
- ¾ cup ditalini

Warm the oil in a 4-quart pot over medium-high heat for 1 minute. Coat the chicken with the pepper. Add chicken, garlic, and shallots to the pot, and sauté until the chicken is lightly browned, about 5 minutes.

Stir in the broth, beans, carrots, celery, bay leaves, and lemon thyme. Cover the pot, and bring the mixture to a boil. Reduce the heat, and simmer for 10 minutes. Stir in the ditalini and cook the soup until the pasta is al dente, 10 to 12 minutes. Discard the bay leaves.

Per serving: 364 calories, 4.1 g fat, 0.9 g saturated fat, 48 mg cholesterol, 209 mg sodium, 8.6 g dietary fiber.

Quick cooking tip: Can't find any fresh lemon thyme? Use regular thyme and add ¼ teaspoon lemon peel.

Chicken Noodle Soup with Fresh Tomatoes

Carrots reign in many traditional chicken-noodle soups; here, tomatoes rule. I think you'll like the perky, unconventional touch.

Makes: 4 servings

- 2 pounds ripe tomatoes
- 1 teaspoon olive oil
- ¾ pound boneless, skinless chicken breasts, cut into ½-inch chunks
- ¼ teaspoon white pepper
- 1 teaspoon thyme leaves
- 4 cloves garlic, crushed
- 1 can (14 ounces) fat-free chicken broth
- 1 teaspoon white wine vinegar
- 1 cup medium egg noodles
- 1 cup frozen peas

Peel and seed the tomatoes, reserving the juice. Cut the tomatoes into small chunks.

Warm the oil in a 4-quart pot over medium-high heat. Coat the chicken with the pepper, thyme, and garlic. Add the chicken to the pot, and sauté until the pieces are lightly browned, about 5 minutes.

Stir in the broth, vinegar, and tomatoes. Cover the pot, and bring the mixture to a boil. Reduce the heat, and simmer for 10 minutes. Add the reserved tomato juice if the soup is too thick.

Stir in the noodles and peas, and cook until the noodles are al dente and the peas are tender, about 5 minutes.

Per serving: 265 calories, 3.6 g fat, 0.7 g saturated fat, 28 mg cholesterol, 119 mg sodium, 5.5 g dietary fiber.

Quick cooking tip: For directions on peeling and seeding tomatoes, see the quick cooking tip under Chunky Cream of Tomato Soup with Tarragon.

Chicken Soupe au Pistou

True to its Provençale heritage, this vegetable-packed chicken soup gets its wonderful garlic flavor from pistou, the French version of the Italian pesto sauce.

Makes: 6 servings

- 2 cans (14 ounces each) fat-free chicken broth
- ¾ pound boneless, skinless chicken breast, cut into ½-inch cubes
- 1 large potato, cut into ½-inch cubes
- 2 carrots, diced
- 1 leek, white part only, thinly sliced
- ¼ teaspoon white pepper
- ¼ cup snipped fresh basil
- 4 cloves garlic, crushed
- 2 teaspoons olive oil
- 1 tomato, quartered and sliced
- 1 medium zucchini, quartered and sliced
- ¼ cup grated Romano cheese

Combine the broth, chicken, potatoes, carrots, leeks, and pepper in a 4-quart pot. Cover the pot, and bring the mixture to a boil. Reduce the heat, and simmer the mixture for 12 minutes.

In the meantime, make the *pistou:* Combine the basil, garlic, and oil in a small bowl.

Add the tomato and zucchini to the chicken mixture in the pot, and simmer for 10 minutes. Stir in the *pistou.* Top each serving with the Romano cheese.

Per serving: 210 calories, 4.8 g fat, 1.5 g saturated fat, 51 mg cholesterol, 216 mg sodium, 2.8 g dietary fiber.

Quick cooking tip: Purple basil, if it's available to you, looks very pretty in this soup.

Chicken Soup Monterey

Definitely not your run-of-the-mill chicken soup. This version is spiked with smoky mesquite flavoring, and it's got a noticeably rich broth–thanks to Monterey Jack cheese. But don't fret–it's still low in calories, fat, and sodium. Best of all, its flavor is incomparable.

Makes: 4 servings

- 2 cans (14 ounces each) fat-free chicken broth
- 2 large potatoes, peeled and cubed
- 1 celery stalk, sliced
- 2 carrots, sliced
- 1 medium onion, chopped
- 1/8 pound deli smoked chicken breast, diced
- 1/2 cup snipped fresh parsley
- 1/2 teaspoon dried marjoram leaves
- 1/4 teaspoon freshly ground black pepper
- 2/3 cup shredded reduced-fat Monterey Jack cheese
- 1 teaspoon mesquite smoke flavoring

Combine the broth, potatoes, celery, carrots, onions, chicken, parsley, marjoram, and pepper in a 4-quart pot. Cover the pot, and bring the mixture to a boil. Reduce the heat, and simmer until the vegetables are tender, about 15 minutes.

Remove from the heat and stir in the cheese and smoke flavoring.

Per serving: 229 calories, 3 g fat, 1.1 g saturated fat, 20 mg cholesterol, 221 mg sodium, 4 g dietary fiber.

Easy Tortilla Soup with Chicken

I first savored this nippy soup during a quick trip to Mexico City. This version includes chicken and tomatoes, and is hearty enough to be a meal in itself.

Makes: 4 servings

> 1 teaspoon olive oil
>
> 1 pound boneless, skinless chicken breasts,
>   cut into ½-inch cubes
>
> 2 medium onions, finely chopped
>
> 4 cloves garlic, minced
>
> 4 cups crushed tomatoes
>
> 3 cups chicken broth
>
> 1 yellow chili pepper, seeded and minced
>
> 2 tablespoons snipped fresh parsley
>
> 8 baked tortilla chips, crushed
>
> ¾ cup shredded Monterey Jack cheese

Warm the oil in a 4-quart pot over medium-high heat for 1 minute. Add the chicken, onions, and garlic, and sauté the mixture until the chicken is browned and the onions are translucent, 5 to 6 minutes.

Stir in the tomatoes, broth, peppers, and parsley. Cover the pot, and bring the mixture to a boil. Reduce the heat, and simmer for 20 minutes. Top each serving with the tortilla chips and Monterey Jack cheese.

Per serving: 357 calories, 8 g fat, 2.5 g saturated fat, 104 mg cholesterol, 329 mg sodium, 3.9 g dietary fiber.

Quick cooking tip: To make your own baked tortilla chips, cut 2 flour or corn tortillas into 1-inch-wide strips. Place the strips on a baking sheet and mist them with cooking spray. Broil them until they're lightly browned, 3 to 5 minutes.

Lemon Chicken and
Wild Pecan Rice Soup

A twist of lemon gives this fuss-free and fast chicken soup a fresh and updated taste.

Makes: 4 servings

2 cans (14 ounces each) fat-free chicken broth

½ pound boneless, skinless chicken breasts, cut into ½-inch cubes

½ cup wild pecan rice

1 celery stalk, thinly sliced

1 medium onion, cut into thin wedges

1 carrot, thinly sliced

1 teaspoon thyme

juice of ½ lemon

½ teaspoon grated lemon peel

¼ teaspoon crushed red pepper flakes

Combine the broth, chicken, rice, celery, onions, carrots, and thyme in a 4-quart pot. Cover the pot, and bring the mixture to a boil. Reduce the heat, and simmer for 30 minutes.

Stir in the lemon juice, lemon peel, and pepper flakes. Cook for 1 minute more.

Per serving: 213 calories, 2.4 g fat, 0.6 g saturated fat, 48 mg cholesterol, 200 mg sodium, 2.7 g dietary fiber.

Quick cooking tip: To squeeze the most from a lemon, grate the peel; then juice the pulp.

Mesquite Chicken Soup

Green tomatoes are the surprise ingredient in this Southwest-inspired soup. Serve it often; it goes together in a flash.

Makes: 4 servings

2 teaspoons olive oil

¾ pound boneless, skinless chicken breasts, cut into ½-inch cubes

1 medium onion, chopped

2 cans (14 ounces each) fat-free chicken broth

½ pound green tomatoes, quartered and sliced

½ cup canned black beans, rinsed and drained

½ cup pinto beans, rinsed and drained

1 small mild green chili, chopped

½ teaspoon cumin seeds

¼ teaspoon freshly ground black pepper

1 teaspoon mesquite smoke flavoring

¼ cup snipped fresh sage

Warm the oil in a 4-quart pot over medium-high heat for 1 minute. Add the chicken and onions, and sauté until the chicken is lightly browned, about 6 minutes. Stir in the broth, tomatoes, black beans, pinto beans, chilies, cumin, and black pepper. Cover the pot, and bring the mixture to a boil. Reduce the heat, and simmer for 15 minutes.

Stir in the mesquite. Top each serving with the sage.

Per serving: 297 calories, 8.3 g fat, 1.6 g saturated fat, 72 mg cholesterol, 211 mg sodium, 5.1 g dietary fiber.

Quick cooking tip: Chilies that would be good in this soup include Anaheim and Serrano.

Asian-Style Turkey Soup

Chinese five-spice powder gives this exuberant soup its sensational flavor kick. Inspiration for it came from a family-favorite stir-fry. It features turkey, rice, broccoli, and red sweet peppers.

Makes: 4 servings

- 1 pound turkey breast slices, cut into ½-inch strips
- 2 cans (14 ounces each) fat-free chicken broth
- ¼ cup long-grain rice
- 1 tablespoon grated gingerroot
- 2 teaspoons reduced-sodium teriyaki sauce
- ½ teaspoon Chinese five-spice powder
- 2 scallions (white part only), chopped
- 1 cup broccoli florets
- 1 red sweet pepper, chopped

Combine the turkey, broth, rice, and gingerroot. Cover the pot, and bring the mixture to a boil. Reduce the heat; simmer for 15 minutes.

Add the teriyaki, five-spice powder, scallions, broccoli, and pepper. Simmer the soup for 5 minutes.

Per serving: 243 calories, 1.1 g fat, 0.3 g saturated fat, 94 mg cholesterol, 308 mg sodium, 1.5 g dietary fiber.

Quick cooking tip: Here's an easy way to store extra gingerroot: Peel the root and cut it into 1-inch-thick slices. Place the pieces in a freezer-proof, self-sealing bag, and freeze. To use a piece, remove it from the freezer, let it sit at room temperature for 3 to 5 minutes, and mince it. Each piece equals about 1 tablespoon when minced.

Harvest Turkey Soup

When only a classic, home-style soup will suit, give this one a shot. Butternut squash and cloves give it a new twist. A dab of butter adds unexpected richness.

Makes: 4 servings

 1 teaspoon olive oil

 1 pound turkey breast cutlets, cut into ½-inch pieces

 3 shallots, sliced

 2 cans (14 ounces each) fat-free chicken broth

 1 cup water

 2 medium red potatoes, cut into ½-inch cubes

 1 pound butternut squash, peeled and cut into ½-inch cubes

 ½ teaspoon thyme leaves

 2 whole cloves

 1 teaspoon butter

Warm the oil in a 4-quart pot over medium-high heat for 1 minute. Add the turkey and shallots, and sauté until the turkey is lightly browned.

Stir in the broth, water, potatoes, squash, and thyme. Place the cloves in a mesh tea ball or tie them in cheesecloth. Add the cloves to the pot. Cover the pot, and bring the mixture to a boil. Reduce the heat, and simmer until the turkey is cooked through and the potatoes and squash are tender, about 15 minutes. Discard the cloves. Stir in the butter.

Per serving: 324 calories, 3.2 g fat, 1.1 g saturated fat, 97 mg cholesterol, 224 mg sodium, 4.9 g dietary fiber.

Smoky Tenderloin Soup

Impress family and friends with this fast, no-hassle soup of turkey, tomatoes, and beans. Its flavors are delightfully smoky and complex, thanks to bottled hickory smoke flavoring.

Makes: 4 servings

2 teaspoons canola oil

1 pound turkey tenderloin, cut into short strips

1 medium red onion, chopped

2 cans (14 ounces each) fat-free chicken broth

1 can (15 ounces) great northern beans, rinsed and drained

1 can (15 ounces) diced tomatoes

2 stalks celery, sliced

2 teaspoons white wine vinegar

¼ teaspoon white pepper

1 teaspoon hickory smoke flavor

½ cup snipped fresh cilantro

Warm the oil in a 4-quart pot over medium-high heat for 1 minute. Add the turkey and onions, and sauté until the pieces are lightly browned, about 5 minutes.

Stir in the broth, beans, tomatoes, celery, vinegar, and pepper. Cover the pot, and bring the mixture to a boil. Reduce the heat, and simmer until the vegetables are tender and the turkey is cooked through, about 15 minutes.

Stir in the smoke flavoring. Top each serving with the cilantro.

Per serving: 390 calories, 6.4 g fat, 1 g saturated fat, 94 mg cholesterol, 232 mg sodium, 9.8 g dietary fiber.

Quick cooking tip: If your market is temporarily out of turkey tenderloin, substitute turkey cutlets or slices.

Sweet Italian Sausage
Soup with Peppers

Can't decide whether to have a sausage and pepper sandwich or a heartwarming soup? Then have the best of each. This smart soup is packed with flavor and brimming with sausage, tomatoes, and colorful peppers.

Makes: 6 servings

½ pound sweet Italian turkey sausage, sliced

1 large onion, chopped

2 cloves garlic, minced

2 cans (14 ounces each) fat-free broth

½ pound red potatoes, chopped

½ teaspoon fennel seeds

¼ teaspoon freshly ground black pepper

1 can (14 ounces) stewed tomatoes, cut up

½ green sweet pepper, chopped

½ yellow pepper, chopped

Warm a nonstick skillet over medium-high heat for 1 minute. Add the sausage, and cook it for 10 minutes. Add the onions and garlic, and sauté the mixture until the onions are translucent, about 3 minutes. Transfer the sausage, onions, and garlic to a 4-quart pot.

Stir in the broth, potatoes, fennel, and black pepper. Cover the pot, and bring the mixture to a boil. Reduce the heat, and simmer for 15 minutes. Stir in tomatoes, green peppers, and yellow peppers. Simmer soup for 5 minutes.

Per serving: 146 calories, 3.1 g fat, 0.9 g saturated fat, 24 mg cholesterol, 481 mg sodium, 2.2 g dietary fiber.

Quick cooking tip: Watching your fat intake? Then be sure to pick up a package of Italian turkey sausage. It has much less fat than the standard pork variety.

Turkey Soup with Acini di Pepe

Get ready for some really good eating. This extra-easy soup is a family favorite featuring turkey, pasta, peas, and tomatoes. A hint of yellow comes from turmeric.

Makes: 4 servings

> 1 teaspoon olive oil
>
> 1 pound turkey breast strips
>
> 1 onion, chopped
>
> 2 stalks celery, thinly sliced
>
> 4 cloves garlic, chopped
>
> 4 cups fat-free chicken broth
>
> ⅛ teaspoon turmeric
>
> 1 lemon thyme sprig or 1 teaspoon thyme
>
> ⅓ cup acini di pepe pasta
>
> 1 cup frozen peas
>
> 2 cups chopped tomatoes
>
> ¼ teaspoon freshly ground black pepper

Warm the oil in a 4-quart pot over medium-high heat for 1 minute. Add the turkey, and cook it until the pieces are lightly browned, 4 to 5 minutes. Stir in the onions, celery, and garlic, and sauté until the onions are translucent. Stir in the broth, turmeric, and lemon thyme. Cover the pot, and bring the mixture to a boil. Reduce the heat, and simmer for 10 minutes.

Stir in the acini di pepe, and cook for 10 minutes. Stir in the peas, tomatoes, and black pepper. Cook until the pasta is al dente and the vegetables are tender, about 4 minutes. Discard the lemon thyme.

Per serving: 306 calories, 2.6 g fat, 0.5 g saturated fat, 94 mg cholesterol, 259 mg sodium, 4.7 g dietary fiber.

Quick cooking tip: Can't find any turkey breast strips? Then get breast slices or cutlets and cut them into thin 1-inch long strips.

Winter-White Vegetable and Turkey Soup

Got some potatoes, turnips, white beans, and leftover roast turkey breast? Turn them into this tantalizing soup. For color and texture contrasts, serve it with a crisp green salad and crunchy croutons.

Makes: 6 servings

1 teaspoon olive oil

1 medium onion, chopped

4 cloves garlic, chopped

2 cans (14 ounces each) fat-free chicken broth

2 potatoes, peeled and cut into ½-inch cubes

1 white turnip, peeled and cut into ½-inch cubes

1 small yellow squash, quartered and sliced

1 can (15 ounces) cannellini beans, rinsed and drained

¼ pound cooked turkey breast, cut into 1-inch cubes

¼ teaspoon white pepper

1 teaspoon dried basil leaves

snipped parsley, for garnish

Warm the oil in a 4-quart pot over medium-high heat for 1 minute. Add the onions and garlic and sauté them until the onions begin to brown. Pour in the broth.

Stir in the potatoes, turnips, squash, beans, turkey, pepper, and basil. Cover the pot, and bring the mixture to a boil. Reduce the heat, and simmer until the vegetables are tender, 15 to 18 minutes.

Remove the pot from the heat. Using a slotted spoon, transfer half the vegetables and turkey to a bowl. Cover the bowl with foil to keep the ingredients warm.

Using a hand-held immersion blender, puree the vegetables and turkey in the pot. Return the reserved vegetables and turkey to the pot. Serve the soup garnished with parsley.

Per serving: 215 calories, 2 g fat, 0.4 g saturated fat, 16 mg cholesterol, 127 mg sodium, 6.9 g dietary fiber.

Quick cooking tip: If you don't have leftover turkey, use deli turkey.

Quick Matzoh Ball Soup

Matzoh ball soup is traditionally enjoyed at the Passover seder, but it's a treat anytime. This version is delicately seasoned with onions, nutmeg, and fresh parsley and is quick to prepare.

Makes: 4 servings

½ cup fat-free egg substitute, lightly beaten

1 teaspoon olive oil

2 tablespoons water

½ teaspoon dried minced onions

⅛ teaspoon nutmeg

1 tablespoon fresh minced parsley

⅛ teaspoon white pepper

½ cup matzoh meal

4 cups fat-free chicken broth

Combine the egg substitute, oil, water, onions, nutmeg, parsley, and pepper in a bowl. Add the matzoh meal and mix well. Cover the bowl, and refrigerate for 15 minutes.

Meanwhile, bring the broth to a simmer in a 4-quart pot.

Form the matzoh mixture into 1-inch balls. Drop the balls into the broth and cook for 20 minutes.

Per serving: 115 calories, 1.2 g fat, 0.2 g saturated fat, 0 mg cholesterol, 220 mg sodium, 0.6 g dietary fiber.

Basically Beef and Other Meats

Beef Noodle Soup Bolognese

Ladle up matchless gourmet flavor with this captivating soup. Traditional Bolognese, named after the rich culinary style of Bologna, Italy, refers to a flavorful meat and vegetable sauce that's often served over pasta. This dish simmers the noodles right along with the beef, prosciutto, mushrooms and tomatoes.

Makes: 4 servings

1 teaspoon butter

1 large onion, chopped

2 ounces prosciutto, chopped

1 teaspoon olive oil

¾ pound ground sirloin

1 cup white mushrooms, chopped

4 cups fat-free beef broth

1 can (15 ounces) diced tomatoes

4 ounces wide egg noodles

2 teaspoons no-salt-added tomato paste

½ teaspoon freshly ground black pepper

1 cup garlic croutons

Melt the butter in a 4-quart pot. Add the onions, prosciutto, and oil, and cook them until the onions are golden, about 5 minutes. Add the sirloin and the mushrooms, and cook until the meat is browned and crumbly, about 8 minutes, stirring occasionally. Drain off excess liquid.

Stir in the broth, tomatoes, noodles, tomato paste, and pepper. Cover the pot, and bring the mixture to a boil. Reduce the heat, and simmer until the noodles are al dente, 8 to 10 minutes. Top each serving with the croutons.

Per serving: 395 calories, 9.3 g fat, 3 g saturated fat, 67 mg cholesterol, 432 mg sodium, 3.6 g dietary fiber.

Quick cooking tip: For directions on making your own croutons, see the quick cooking tip under French Onion Soup.

Goulash Soup

My love affair with goulash soup began 10 years ago in a casual German eatery, and time hasn't lessened my enthusiasm for this robust noodle 'n' beef dish. In this quick version, cocoa and a generous spoonful of paprika give the tomato-beef broth a rich depth of flavor and color.

Makes: 6 servings

- 1 teaspoon olive oil
- ¾ pound beef round roast
- 1 large onion, cut into rings
- 2 cups sliced white mushrooms
- 3 cans (14 ounces each) fat-free beef broth
- 1 can (15 ounces) stewed tomatoes, cut up
- 1 teaspoon cocoa
- 4 ounces Hungarian egg noodles *(kluski)*
- 1 tablespoon paprika
- 2 teaspoons caraway seeds

Trim visible fat from the beef and tenderize it with a meat mallet. Cut into ½-inch cubes.

Warm the oil in a 4-quart pot over medium-high heat for 1 minute. Add the beef and sauté until it is lightly browned, about 6 minutes. Add the onions and mushrooms and sauté until the onions are translucent, about 3 minutes.

Stir in the broth, tomatoes, and cocoa. Cover the pot, and bring the mixture to a boil. Reduce the heat, and simmer for 10 minutes. Stir in the noodles and paprika, and simmer for 18 minutes. Top each serving with the caraway seeds.

Per serving: 216 calories, 4.6 g fat, 1.2 g saturated fat, 26 mg cholesterol, 179 mg sodium, 2.4 g dietary fiber.

Quick cooking tip: If you can't find the Hungarian noodles, substitute thin egg noodles.

Mini-Meatball Soup with Alphabet Pasta

Wow hungry diners with this exceptional yet easy soup of meatballs, Swiss chard, and tiny pasta. Provolone cheese provides richness and subtle smoky flavor.

Makes: 4 servings

- ½ pound ground round (beef)
- ½ cup quick-cooking oats
- 3 tablespoons dried minced onions
- 2 teaspoons oregano
- 1 egg white
- 2 cans (14 ounces each) fat-free chicken broth
- 2 carrots, thinly sliced
- 2 ounces alphabet pasta
- 2 cups torn Swiss chard greens
- ½ cup grated Provolone cheese

Combine the beef, oats, 2 teaspoons onions, ½ teaspoon oregano, and the egg white. Form ½-inch-diameter meatballs. (The mixture should make about 32.) Warm a nonstick skillet over medium-high heat for 1 minute. Add the meatballs, and cook them until they are brown on all sides, about 10 minutes, turning them occasionally.

Meanwhile, combine the broth, carrots, remaining onions, and remaining oregano in a 4-quart pot. Cover the pot, and bring the mixture to a boil. Reduce the heat, and simmer for 5 minutes. Add the meatballs and pasta, and simmer until the pasta is al dente, 8 to 10 minutes. Stir in the chard and Provolone.

Per serving: 305 calories, 5.9 g fat, 2.6 g saturated fat, 56 mg cholesterol, 388 mg sodium, 4.5 g dietary fiber.

Quick cooking tip: Form *firm* meatballs so they hold together during cooking.

Savory Steak and Sweet Potato Soup

Instead of the usual potatoes and carrots, this scrumptious beef soup relies on sweet potatoes for body, flavor and color. Peas provide a bright burst of contrasting color.

Makes: 4 servings

½ teaspoon freshly ground black pepper

2 tablespoons snipped fresh sage

2 teaspoons olive oil

½ pound round steak, cut into ½-inch cubes

1 medium Spanish onion, chopped

2 cans (14 ounces each) fat-free beef broth

2 cups shredded peeled sweet potato

¼ cup dry red wine

1 cup frozen peas

½ teaspoon paprika

Combine the pepper and sage. Coat the beef cubes with 1 teaspoon olive oil. Rub the pepper–sage mixture over the beef. Warm the remaining 1 teaspoon oil in a 4-quart pot. Add the beef and onions, and sauté them until the beef is lightly browned, about 5 minutes.

Stir in the broth, sweet potato, and wine. Cover the pot, and bring the mixture to a boil. Reduce the heat, and simmer for 15 minutes. Stir in the peas and simmer the soup for 5 minutes. Top each serving with the paprika.

Per serving: 288 calories, 5.4 g fat, 1.3 g saturated fat, 48 mg cholesterol, 177 mg sodium, 4.5 g dietary fiber.

Quick cooking tip: Use the moist, red (deep orange) variety of sweet potato for this recipe.

Borscht with Veal Sausage

Spicy veal sausage brings zip to this fast version of a traditional Russian beet soup. Serve it hot with a dollop of sour cream.

Makes: 4 servings

- 2 cups canned diced beets with liquid
- 2 cans (14 ounces each) fat-free beef broth
- 1 cup shredded carrots
- 1 cup coarsely chopped red cabbage
- 1 medium onion, chopped
- 4 ounces cooked veal sausage, chopped
- ½ cup shredded white turnip
- 1 tablespoon tomato paste
- 2 teaspoons red wine vinegar
- ½ teaspoon sugar
- ½ teaspoon freshly ground black pepper
- ½ cup nonfat sour cream

Combine the beets, broth, carrots, cabbage, onions, sausage, turnips, tomato paste, vinegar, sugar, and pepper in a 4-quart pot. Cover the pot, and bring the mixture to a boil. Reduce the heat, and simmer for 15 minutes.

Remove the pot from the heat. Using a hand-held immersion blender, process the mixture until it is partially pureed. Top each serving with a swirl of the sour cream.

Per serving: 135 calories, 1.9 g fat, 0.7 g saturated fat, 31 mg cholesterol, 245 mg sodium, 4.7 g dietary fiber.

Quick cooking tip: For maximum black pepper flavor, always use the freshly ground variety. The preground stuff quickly loses its flavor and leaves only its bite.

Quick Vegetable and Veal Sausage Soup

A handful of beans, some diced potatoes and carrots, and a little veal sausage. You can throw this hearty soup together in no time flat—no kidding. It's ready to eat after just 15 minutes of simmering. What more could you want? Great flavor? It's here.

Makes: 4 servings

- 2 cans (14 ounces each) fat-free chicken broth
- 2 medium red potatoes, diced
- 1 can (15 ounces) cannellini beans, rinsed and drained
- ⅛ pound cooked veal sausage, chopped
- 1 carrot, diced
- 1 celery stalk, chopped
- 1 medium onion, chopped
- 4 cloves garlic, chopped
- ½ teaspoon herbes de Provence
- ¼ teaspoon freshly ground black pepper
- ¼ cup snipped fresh parsley, for garnish

Combine the broth, potatoes, beans, sausage, carrots, celery, onions, garlic, herbes de Provence, and pepper in a 4-quart pot. Cover the pot, and bring the mixture to a boil. Reduce the heat, and simmer until the vegetables are tender, about 15 minutes.

Transfer half the vegetables and sausage to a bowl. Using a hand-held immersion blender, puree the mixture. Return it to the pot. Top each serving with parsley.

Per serving: 216 calories, 1.4 g fat, 0.4 g saturated fat, 11 mg cholesterol, 175 mg sodium, 7.7 g dietary fiber.

Veal Scallops with Mushroom Caps

Veal scallops, shallots, white wine, mushrooms—such trendy ingredients plus no-hassle preparation redefine home-style soup. It's light yet satisfying. It's robust yet refined. It's delicious.

Makes: 4 servings

2 teaspoons olive oil

1 pound veal scallops, about ⅛ inch thick

4 ounces mushroom caps, quartered if large

2 shallots, thinly sliced

2 cloves garlic, chopped

2 cans (14 ounces each) fat-free chicken broth

½ cup dry white wine, such as Chardonnay

½ teaspoon white pepper

½ teaspoon marjoram leaves

¼ cup roasted red peppers, chopped

¼ cup snipped fresh parsley

Heat the oil in a 4-quart pot over medium-high heat for 1 minute. Add the veal, mushrooms, shallots, and garlic, and sauté until the veal is no longer pink, 3 to 7 minutes.

Stir in the broth, wine, and white pepper. Cover the pot, and bring the mixture to a boil. Reduce the heat, and simmer for 10 minutes. Stir in the marjoram. Top each serving with the red peppers and parsley.

Per serving: 240 calories, 8 g fat, 1.9 g saturated fat, 99 mg cholesterol, 222 mg sodium, 1 g dietary fiber.

Quick cooking tip: When veal scallops are hard to find, substitute very thin slices of veal, and cut them into bite-size pieces.

Rustic Lamb Soup
with Adzuki Beans

Enjoy the classic pairing of rosemary and lamb in this 30-minute soup, which also sports potatoes, turnips, beans, and onions.

Makes: 4 servings

2 teaspoons dried rosemary

½ teaspoon freshly ground black pepper

½ pound lean lamb shoulder, cut into ½-inch cubes

1 teaspoon olive oil

1 medium onion, thinly sliced

2½ cups fat-free beef broth

1 turnip, cut into ½-inch cubes

1 medium red potato, cut into ½-inch cubes

¾ cup rinsed and drained canned adzuki beans

1 cup torn sorrel leaves

Combine the rosemary and pepper. Sprinkle the seasonings over the lamb.

Warm the oil in a 4-quart pot over medium-high heat for 1 minute. Add the lamb and onions, and sauté until the lamb is lightly browned, about 5 minutes.

Stir in the broth, turnips, potatoes, and beans. Cover the pot, and bring the mixture to a boil. Reduce the heat, and simmer until the vegetables are tender, about 15 minutes. Stir in the sorrel.

Per serving: 253 calories, 6.7 g fat, 2.2 g saturated fat, 52 mg cholesterol, 183 mg sodium, 3.2 g dietary fiber.

Quick cooking tip: To bring out rosemary's delightful piney essence, crush the leaves between your fingers before using them.

Bratwurst and Beer Soup

Here's to a great Germanfest! This lively and hearty soup is perfect for spur-of-the-moment supping, even if you haven't invited a crowd.

Makes: 4 servings

1 teaspoon olive oil

¼ pound cooked bratwurst, halved and sliced

2 cups fat-free beef broth

2 leeks, white part only, sliced

1 large potato, peeled and cut into ½-inch cubes

¼ teaspoon white pepper

1 red sweet pepper, chopped

1 cup nonalcoholic beer

¼ cup snipped fresh chives

Warm the oil in a 4-quart pot over medium-high heat for 1 minute. Add the bratwurst, and sauté until they're lightly browned. Transfer them to a bowl; cover with foil to keep the sausage warm.

Combine the broth, leeks, potatoes, and pepper in the same 4-quart pot. Cover the pot, and bring the mixture to a boil. Reduce the heat, and simmer until the potatoes are tender, about 15 minutes. Transfer half the mixture to a bowl; cover with foil to keep the vegetables warm.

Using a potato masher, mash the vegetables remaining in the pot. Stir in the bratwurst and reserved vegetables. Stir in the sweet pepper and beer. Simmer the soup for 5 minutes. Top each serving with the chives.

Per serving: 199 calories, 8.8 g fat, 2.8 g saturated fat, 17 mg cholesterol, 253 mg sodium, 2.3 g dietary fiber.

Quick cooking tip: Before slicing the leeks, swish them in plenty of cold water to remove the sand that's trapped between the layers.

Chinese Pork Noodle Soup

Bok choy, pork, Chinese noodles, sesame oil, soy sauce—all add up to a captivating soup with tons of Asian-style flavor.

Makes: 4 servings

½ pound center cut pork loin

1 teaspoon sesame oil

6 mushroom caps, sliced

4 cups fat-free chicken broth

1 tablespoon dry sherry

2 teaspoons reduced-sodium soy sauce

1 cup sliced bok choy

2 cups torn spinach leaves

2 scallions, sliced

4 ounces Chinese wheat noodles

2 cups bean sprouts

Using a meat mallet, pound the pork to tenderize it. Cut the pork into thin 1-inch-long strips. Warm the oil in a skillet over medium-high heat for 1 minute. Add the pork and mushrooms, and sauté until the pork is lightly browned.

Transfer the mixture to a 4-quart pot, and add the broth, sherry, soy sauce, bok choy, spinach, and scallions. Cover the pot, and bring the mixture to a boil. Reduce the heat, and simmer for 4 minutes.

Stir in the noodles and sprouts, and cook the soup for 3 minutes more.

Per serving: 297 calories, 6.4 g fat, 1.9 g saturated fat, 47 mg cholesterol, 323 mg sodium, 2.9 g dietary fiber.

Quick cooking tip: Can't find any Chinese noodles? Then substitute angel hair pasta.

Kielbasa with Roasted Pepper Soup

Wow a group of hungry friends with this tasty soup. It's packed with potatoes, onions, and flavorful Polish kielbasa, and topped with roasted peppers.

Makes: 4 servings

- 1 teaspoon olive oil
- ¼ pound cooked kielbasa, halved and sliced
- 1 large onion, chopped
- 2 cans (14 ounces each) fat-free chicken broth
- 1 large potato, peeled and diced
- 1 celery stalk, sliced
- 1 teaspoon white wine vinegar
- ½ teaspoon dried thyme leaves
- ¼ teaspoon lemon pepper
- ¼ cup diced roasted red peppers, for garnish

Warm the oil in a 4-quart pot over medium-high heat for 1 minute. Add the kielbasa and onion, and sauté the mixture until the onion begins to brown, about 6 minutes. Pour in the broth. Add the potatoes, celery, vinegar, thyme, and lemon pepper.

Cover the pot, and bring the mixture to a boil. Reduce the heat, and simmer until the vegetables are tender, about 15 minutes. Top each serving with the red peppers.

Per serving: 162 calories, 2.5 g fat, 0.6 g saturated fat, 13 mg cholesterol, 358 mg sodium, 2.7 g dietary fiber.

Quick cooking tip: To reduce prep time, replace freshly roasted red peppers with the variety from a jar.

Pasta, Peas, and Pork Soup

Simplicity makes this homey soup a superb last-minute supper choice. The dish has few requirements: everyday ingredients, 4 simple steps, and just 30 minutes to cook.

Makes: 4 servings

1 teaspoon olive oil

¾ pound boneless, center cut pork chops, trimmed of fat and cut into ½-inch cubes

4 cloves garlic, crushed

1 large onion, chopped

5 cups water

4 envelopes low-sodium beef bouillon powder

¼ teaspoon ground celery seeds

2 teaspoons Worcestershire sauce

¼ teaspoon white pepper

1 cup ditalini

1 cup peas

Warm the oil in a 4-quart pot over medium-high heat for 1 minute. Add the pork and sauté until the pieces are no longer pink, about 10 minutes. Add the onions and garlic, and sauté the mixture until the onions are lightly browned, about 10 minutes.

Stir in the water, bouillon, celery seeds, Worcestershire sauce, and pepper. Cover the pot, and bring the mixture to a boil. Stir in the pasta. Reduce the heat, and simmer the mixture for 10 minutes. Stir in the peas and cook the soup until the pasta is al dente and the peas are tender, 4 to 5 minutes.

Per serving: 352 calories, 8.6 g fat, 2.8 g saturated fat, 70 mg cholesterol, 124 mg sodium, 4 g dietary fiber.

Zuppa di Giorno

Hot Italian sausage and a few pinches of fennel bring intense flavor to this carefree soup. I've used fusilli, but ziti or rotini would soak up the broth's flavors just as nicely.

Makes: 6 servings

¼ pound hot Italian sausage

4 cups fat-free chicken broth

2 cups frozen baby lima beans

2 carrots, sliced

1 large onion, chopped

1 small zucchini, thin sliced

1 bay leaf

½ teaspoon fennel seeds, crushed

¼ teaspoon thyme

¼ teaspoon freshly ground black pepper

8 ounces fusilli

Sauté the sausage in a nonstick skillet until browned, about 8 minutes. Transfer it to a cutting board and chop into small pieces.

In a 4-quart pot, combine the broth, beans, carrots, onions, zucchini, bay leaf, fennel seeds, thyme, and pepper. Cover the pot, and bring the mixture to a boil. Reduce the heat, and simmer until the vegetables are tender, 15 to 20 minutes.

Stir in the fusilli. Simmer until the pasta is al dente, about 10 minutes. Discard the bay leaf.

Per serving: 310 calories, 4.6 g fat, 1.4 g saturated fat, 11 mg cholesterol, 257 mg sodium, 7.3 g dietary fiber.

Quick cooking tip: Got a slow cooker? Here's your chance to use it. Simply sauté the sausage in a nonstick skillet and chop it into small pieces. Combine the sausage and all remaining ingredients except the fusilli in an electric slow cooker. Cover the cooker, and cook on LOW for 5 to 7 hours. Stir in the fusilli; cook until al dente, about 40 minutes.

White Bean and Ham Soup

A little white cheddar cheese smoothes out the earthiness of this singular soup. Serve it with croutons or crusty bread to sop up the flavorful broth.

Makes: 6 servings

2 cans (14 ounces each) fat-free chicken broth

1 can (15 ounces) great northern beans, rinsed and drained

2 large potatoes, peeled and cubed

1 turnip, peeled and cubed

1 celery stalk, sliced

1 small onion, chopped

⅛ pound cooked lean deli ham, chopped

2 cloves garlic, chopped

1 teaspoon white wine vinegar

¼ teaspoon white pepper

¼ teaspoon ground dried savory

½ cup reduced-fat white cheddar cheese

paprika, for garnish

Combine the broth, beans, potatoes, turnips, celery, onions, ham, garlic, vinegar, pepper, and savory in a 4-quart pot. Cover the pot, and bring the mixture to a boil. Reduce the heat, and simmer until the vegetables are tender, about 15 minutes.

Remove the soup from the heat. Using a hand-held immersion blender, coarsely partially puree the vegetables. Stir in the cheddar. Serve the soup garnished with the paprika.

Per serving: 220 calories, 2.6 g fat, 1.3 g saturated fat, 12 mg cholesterol, 291 mg sodium, 7.3 g dietary fiber.

Soup Accompaniments

Wheat Biscuits with Cream Cheese and Chives

These tender biscuits are extra-easy and 1-2-3 fast because they're drop biscuits, not roll-and-cut biscuits.

Makes: 12 biscuits

nonstick cooking spray

1½ cups unbleached flour

½ cup whole wheat flour

3 teaspoons baking powder

¼ teaspoon salt

2½ tablespoons butter

2½ tablespoons nonfat cream cheese

2 tablespoons snipped fresh chives

¾ cup skim milk

Coat a baking sheet with the spray. Heat oven to 450°F (232°C).

In a medium-size bowl, whisk together the unbleached flour, whole wheat flour, baking powder and salt. Using a pastry blender or two table knives, cut in the butter and cream cheese until the flour mixture resembles coarse crumbs. Stir in the chives. Pour in the milk. Using a fork, mix until the ingredients are just combined.

To form the biscuits, drop the dough by the tablespoonfuls onto the baking sheet. Bake until lightly browned, 10 to 12 minutes. Serve hot.

Per serving: 108 calories, 2.9 g fat, 1.6 g saturated fat, 7.3 mg cholesterol, 199 mg sodium, 0.6 g dietary fiber.

Sesame Bread Sticks

There's something irresistible about warm, freshly baked bread sticks with sesame seeds. These bake up in a hurry.

Makes: 8 bread sticks

   olive-oil cooking spray

   1 tablespoon yellow cornmeal

   8 frozen yeast dough rolls, thawed

   1 teaspoon toasted sesame seeds

Coat a baking sheet with the spray; dust it with the cornmeal.

Stretch and roll each yeast ball into a 12-inch stick; place the sticks on the baking sheet. Mist them with the spray. Sprinkle the sesame seeds over them. Loosely cover the entire sheet with plastic wrap, and let the sticks rest for 20 minutes in a warm spot. Meanwhile, heat oven to 425°F (218°C).

Discard the plastic wrap. Bake the bread sticks until they're golden, about 10 minutes.

Per bread stick: 82 calories, 1.6 g fat, 0.4 g saturated fat, 1.4 mg cholesterol, 137 mg sodium, 0.6 g dietary fiber.

Variations: You may substitute poppy seeds or dried minced onions for the sesame seeds.

Individual Bacon–Cheese Breads

Indulge in the flavors of bacon and cheddar with little worry about fat and cholesterol.

Makes: 8 small breads

nonstick cooking spray

1 tablespoon cornmeal

8 frozen yeast dough rolls, thawed

2 bacon slices, cooked and crumbled

⅛ cup shredded reduced-fat, reduced-sodium cheddar cheese

Coat a baking sheet with the spray; dust it with the cornmeal.

Gently stretch each roll into a 4-inch circle. Mist the top of the dough with the spray. Sprinkle the bacon and cheddar over the dough. Lightly press the seasonings into the dough.

Loosely cover the dough with plastic wrap, and let the breads rest for 20 minutes in a warm place. Meanwhile, heat oven to 425°F (218°C).

Discard the plastic wrap. Bake the bread rounds until they are golden brown, 9 to 11 minutes.

Per bread: 93 calories, 2.4 g fat, 0.7 g saturated fat, 3.4 mg cholesterol, 165 mg sodium, 0.5 g dietary fiber.

Onion–Olive Focaccia

Here's an instant dinner winner that feeds a small crowd; because it's made with refrigerated pizza dough, it goes together in a culinary flash.

Makes: 8 slices

olive-oil cooking spray

1 tablespoon cornmeal

1 package (10 ounces) store-bought refrigerated pizza crust

2 teaspoons crushed garlic

1 small onion, thinly sliced

½ medium red sweet pepper, sliced into thin strips

8 black olives, thinly sliced

Heat oven to 425°F (218°C). Coat a perforated pizza pan with the spray; dust it with the cornmeal.

Gently stretch the dough into a 12-inch-diameter circle. Mist the top of the dough with the spray. Spread the garlic over the dough, and arrange the onions, peppers, and olives on the dough. Bake the focaccia until it is golden brown, 10 to 12 minutes.

Per serving: 108 calories, 1.8 g fat, 0.3 g saturated fat, 0 mg cholesterol, 234 mg sodium, 2.5 g dietary fiber.

Glossary

Acini di pepe: A tiny peppercorn-shaped pasta that gets its name from the Italian for "peppercorn."

Adzuki bean: A small dried legume that's especially popular in Japanese cooking. Adzuki beans have a slightly sweet flavor.

Allspice: Though this spice tastes like a combination of cinnamon, nutmeg and cloves, it's really just one spice, a small, dark-brown berry. Allspice flavors both savory and sweet dishes, and you can buy it whole or ground.

Anchovy: A small silvery fish that's usually filleted, salt-cured, and canned in oil. It is used in small amounts to add intense flavor to hot dishes, sauces, and salad dressings. To remove some of the excess salt, soak anchovies in cool water for 30 minutes, pat them dry with a paper towel, and add them to your recipe. Store leftover anchovies covered with oil in an airtight container in the refrigerator for up to 2 months.

Bisque: A thick, creamy soup that's usually smooth and made with shellfish, especially crab meat, lobster, or shrimp, though it can be made with poultry or vegetables.

Black-eyed pea: Also called a cowpea, this legume is small and beige with an oval black "eye" at the center of its curve. Its texture is mealy; its flavor, earthy. Look for black-eyed peas fresh, frozen, canned, or dried.

Bolognese: This is a thick meat and vegetable sauce that's often served over pasta. The flavor and richness of the sauce may be boosted by wine, milk, or cream. The term "Bolognese" actually refers to the rich cooking style found in Bologna, Italy.

Borscht: a beet soup with origins in Russia and Poland, borscht usually contains meat and fresh vegetables and may be served either hot or cold with a dollop of sour cream.

Bratwurst: Pale, almost white in color, bratwurst is a German sausage made of pork and veal and delightfully seasoned with spices such as coriander, ginger, and nutmeg. It's available fresh and fully cooked.

Broccoflower: A neon green cruciferous vegetable that's a cross between broccoli and cauliflower. It resembles cauliflower, and tastes like a mild version of both its parents. Choose heads with compact florets, bright coloring, and no browning. Store and prepare as you would cauliflower.

Butternut squash: A variety of hard-shelled winter squash that has a beige exterior and a deep orange-colored flesh. Though generally available year round, butternut's peak season starts in early fall and ends in late winter. Purchase butternuts that are heavy for their size and blemish free. Since they don't need refrigeration, you can stash them in a cool, dry, dark spot for a month or more.

Cannellini: These are large white kidney beans popular in Italian soups and salads. They're available in dried and canned forms.

Caper: The flower bud of a Mediterranean shrub, the caper has a prized sour and slightly bitter flavor. Its size ranges from tiny (a French nonpareil variety) to large (an Italian variety that's as big as the end of your little finger). Once picked, the bud is sun-dried, then packed in salt or a vinegar brine. To remove some of the saltiness, rinse capers in cold water before using them. The flower buds of nasturtium, buttercup, marigold and broom are sometimes used as inexpensive substitutes for capers.

Caraway: Small, crescent-shaped seeds with a delightful nutty, anise-like aroma and flavor. The seeds are used extensively in German and Austrian cooking. In the U.S., they're probably best known for flavoring rye bread.

Celery seed: This tiny pungent seed comes from lovage, a cousin to celery. Its flavor is fairly intense, so use the spice, which is available whole or ground, sparingly.

Cellophane noodles: Also called *bean thread noodles, Chinese vermicelli, glass noodles,* and *harusame.* Sold dried in cellophane packages, these noodles are made from mung beans and must be soaked in hot water for a few minutes before they're added to most dishes. Soups represent the occasional exception to the soaking guidelines.

Chickpeas: *See* Garbanzo beans.

Chili powder: A hot, spicy mixture of chili peppers, oregano, cumin, salt, garlic, coriander and cloves. For an intense blend, get one without salt. Chili powder is a mainstay in chilies and other Mexican- and Tex-Mex-style dishes.

Chinese five-spice powder: As its name suggests, this seasoning contains just five spices usually in equal parts: cinnamon, cloves, fennel seed, star anise, and Szechuan peppers. Use it to flavor up Asian-style dishes.

Chinese wheat noodles: Very thin noodles made from wheat, water, salt and, sometimes, eggs. The flavor is nutty and delicate. If you can't find them, substitute angel-hair pasta.

Chowder: A thick, chunky soup that's frequently made with cream-style corn, milk, or tomatoes. Chicken, clam, and other seafood chowders are the most well known.

Cilantro: Also called *Chinese parsley* and *fresh coriander,* cilantro is an herb with small, fragile leaves and a lively, almost musty taste. It's a signature flavor for Caribbean, Latin American, and some Asian cuisines. Choose bunches of leaves with bright lively color and no signs of wilting. Store cilantro, unwashed, in a plastic bag in the refrigerator for up to a week. Wash the leaves just before using them.

Cream-style corn: When commercially prepared, this corn product contains corn, sugar and cornstarch. Homemade cream-style corn is nothing more than the pulp and juice squeezed from corn kernels.

Cumin: A small, amber-colored seed resembling a miniature caraway seed, cumin is a parsley relative. Cumin has an aromatic, pungent, nutty flavor that dominates many Mexican and Indian dishes. You can find whole and ground cumin. If you have access to an Asian market, check out the white and black cumin seeds. The white and amber varieties can be used interchangeably, but the black ones have a more complex, peppery flavor.

Curry powder: Not a single spice, but a blend of up to 20 spices and herbs, including cumin, coriander, red pepper, fenugreek, cinnamon, allspice, fennel, ginger, black pepper, mace, nutmeg, cloves, poppy seeds, sesame seeds, and turmeric. The latter gives the blend its yellow color. To eliminate any raw taste, toast curry powder in a small nonstick skillet before adding it to a recipe. Curry powder is the signature seasoning in all curry dishes.

Dill: This name refers to both dillweed, the feathery leaves of the dill plant, and dillseed, the plant's tan, flat seeds. Both have a refreshing flavor, though dillseed is somewhat sharper. Whenever possible, use fresh dill for perking up salads, vegetables, sauces and vinaigrettes; its flavor is superior to that of dried dillweed. Dillseed is best known for its use in pickling.

Garbanzo beans: Also called chickpeas, garbanzo beans are round, light tan legumes with a firm texture and mild, nutlike flavor. They're used extensively in Middle East dishes such as hummus, a garlic- and lemon-flavored dip served with pita bread pockets. They're available dried and canned.

Ginger: A seasoning with a somewhat sweet aroma, a pungent flavor, and a peppery after-kick, ginger comes in three forms: fresh (a gnarled root), dried and ground (located with the jarred spices), and crystallized (found in small packets with candied fruits). Fresh ginger, which is often called gingerroot, makes a delicious contribution to curries, soups, and Asian-style stir-fries. Dried ginger, which should not be used as a substitute for the fresh version, adds indispensable flavor to gingerbread, gingersnaps, and ginger ale. The crystallized version, which has been cooked in a sugar syrup, jazzes up fruit compotes and the like. Fresh ginger can be stored, tightly wrapped in plastic wrap, in the refrigerator for up to 3 weeks or in the freezer for up to 6 months.

Green tomatoes: Unripe tomatoes.

Gruyère cheese: A slightly assertive, deliciously nutty cheese with teeny holes and an ivory color. Gruyère's flavor rivals that of Swiss cheese; the two can be used interchangeably. Processed Gruyère contains both Emmentaler (a type of Swiss cheese) and Gruyère and has a flavor and texture that's quite different from that of natural Gruyère.

Havarti cheese: A mild, semisoft Danish cheese that's produced in both Denmark and the United States. Made from cow's milk, it has tiny "eyes" and may include flavorings such as caraway, dill, other herbs, and jalapeño peppers. It's available in full-fat and reduced-fat versions.

Herbes de Provence: A commercial blend of six dried herbs, which is typically used in the cuisine of southern France: rosemary, marjoram, thyme, sage, anise seed, and savory. Use it to season chicken, pork, veal, fish, and shrimp dishes.

Hot-pepper sauce: Not a single sauce, but one of many Louisiana-style sauces made from hot chili peppers, vinegar and salt. The heat and flavor vary from brand to brand. Some are relatively mild; others, so scorching that just a drop or two fires up an entire dish. When using a hot sauce for the first time, cautiously add it to soups, stews marinades and other dishes.

Italian herb seasoning: A pleasant herb blend of oregano, basil and thyme, and sometimes red pepper, rosemary and garlic powder. Use the mix to achieve characteristic Italian flavor without measuring out the individual seasonings.

Kielbasa: This is a robust smoked Polish sausage that's usually sold precooked. Most kielbasa is made with pork, though beef is sometimes added. Nowadays, you can also get lower-fat turkey versions. For best flavor, always heat kielbasa before serving it.

Kluski: These are sturdy Hungarian-style egg noodles.

Leek: A member of the lily family and a cousin of garlic and onion, the leek resembles a gigantic scallion. Its flavor and fragrance are mildly onionlike; its texture crunchy. When buying leeks, look for crisp, brightly colored leaves and unblemished white portions. Slender leeks are the most tender. To use leeks, cut off the rootlets and slit the leeks from end to end. Then swish them in cool running water to wash away dirt trapped between the layers.

Lemon pepper: A seasoning blend of black pepper and grated lemon zest. Check the label before buying this blend; it sometimes contains more salt than pepper or lemon.

Lentils: Meaty tasting and packed with protein, lentils are small disk-shaped legumes that come in three varieties: greyish-brown (European), reddish-orange (Egyptian) and yellow. Of the three, the greyish-brown lentils are commonly found in supermarkets; the others can be obtained in Middle Eastern and Indian groceries. Stored at room temperature in a dry place, lentils will keep for a year.

Madeira wine: A fortified wine that's named after the Portuguese island, Madeira. Its color runs from pale golden to rich tawny, and its flavor can be anywhere from quite dry to very sweet.

Marjoram: Also called *sweet marjoram*. A member of the mint family, marjoram has long, oval leaves with a mild oreganolike flavor. To retain its delicate taste, add marjoram to dishes toward the end of cooking.

Marsala: A fortified wine that's imported from Sicily. Its intriguing smoky flavor ranges from sweet to dry.

Mustard greens: These dark leafy greens, a popular must-have in Southern country cooking, have a pungent, almost peppery mustard flavor, and provide a tasty accent when added to green salads and cooked dishes. For top quality, buy them during their peak season: December through March. Look for small crisp leaves with a bright color. To store them, place them in a plastic bag in the refrigerator for

122

up to a week. Rinse and pat them dry immediately before use.

Mustard seeds: Simply put, these are the seeds of mustard plants, peppery greens belonging to the same family as broccoli, brussels sprouts, kale, collards, and kohlrabi. The seeds themselves come in three varieties: black, brown, and yellow, yellow being the most common and most readily available. Left whole or cracked, mustard seeds boost the flavor of potato salad, pickles, relishes, and boiled shrimp.

Nutmeg: A hard, brownish seed with a warm, spicy, sweet flavor. It's sold ground and whole. Expect to get the best flavor from freshly ground nutmeg. Use nutmeg to perk up baked goods, custards, and vegetables, such as potatoes and winter squash.

Orange roughy: A low-fat fish with firm white flesh and mild flavor. Hails from Australia and New Zealand. In the U.S., it's available frozen or thawed.

Paprika: A special variety of red sweet pepper pods that have been ground for use as a seasoning and a garnish. Paprika comes from several parts of the world–Spain, California, South America and Hungary. The Hungarian variety is considered by many to be a standout. After opening paprika, store it in the refrigerator where it'll retain its bright color and flavor longest.

Pasta: A dough (or paste) made with flour and water and, sometimes, eggs. Generally speaking, pasta made with eggs is called *noodles* in the United States. You can make your own pasta or buy it fresh, frozen, or dried. The latter is the most popular, since it's inexpensive and keeps almost indefinitely. Dried pasta comes in at least 600 shapes.

Peppercorns: These are the berries of the pepper plant *(Piper nigrum)* that produces black and white pepper. Black pepper, the most popular, comes from the dried berry *with* its skin; white pepper, which is also dried, comes *minus* the skin. Of the two, white pepper is slightly milder and is a good choice in light-colored sauces where dark specks of black pepper would stand out.

Pepperoni: A highly seasoned beef and pork sausage. Popular in Italy, the sausage is firm, air-dried, and ready to eat. Sliced thinly or chopped coarsely, it makes a delightful addition to many cooked dishes.

Peppers: Crunchy, colorful, flavorful, sweet, hot, versatile, high in vitamin C–such attributes make peppers a favored vegetable in many cuisines: Mexican, Chinese, Thai, Hungarian, to name a few. Though there are scads of pepper varieties, all can be divided into two basic categories—sweet and hot. Here's a brief rundown of several popular and readily available peppers:

> **Bell:** A sweet, bell-shaped pepper that comes in green, red, yellow, orange, brown or purple. They're suitable for stuffing, slicing and dicing. Use them to punch up color, flavor and crunch in just about any soup, stew, casserole, stir-fry or sandwich.
>
> **Cayenne:** A long, thin, sharply pointed hot pepper that's either straight or curled. Generally, cayennes are sold when fully ripe and red in color.
>
> **Jalapeño:** A tapered, 2-inch-long, very hot pepper that's usually sold at the green but mature stage. Used to season sausage, cheeses, and even jellies.
>
> **Pimento (pimiento):** A large, heart-shaped, mild pepper that's usually sold in jars. Thick and meaty, these peppers are ideal for roasting, if you can find them fresh.
>
> **Poblano:** A very dark green, moderately hot pepper that resembles a small bell pepper with a tapered blossom end.

Prosciutto: Usually sold in transparently thin slices, prosciutto, which in Italian means "ham," is a seasoned, salt-cured, and air-dried meat. Connoisseurs often recommend eating it as is. If you do cook it, add it to hot foods at the last minute; prolonged cooking will toughen it.

Provolone cheese: A firm Italian cheese with a mild, smoky flavor and firm texture. Made from cow's milk, Provolone makes an excellent cooking cheese and, when aged, grates nicely for use as a topping.

Romano cheese: A nippy cheese with a light yellow color and hard texture similar to that of Parmesan cheese. Romano is generally grated and often added to Italian-style dishes. For maximum flavor, use it freshly grated.

Rosemary: The green leaves of this aromatic herb resemble pine needles, and many cooks describe its taste as somewhat piny. Chop fresh leaves before using them and crush the dried form with a mortar and pestle. Rosemary is fairly assertive, especially when fresh, so apply it with restraint in vinaigrettes, sauces, lamb and chicken dishes.

Sesame oil: Pressed from sesame seeds, sesame oil comes in two types: light and dark. The light oil is lighter in flavor and color; use it to enhance salad dressings and for sautéing. Reserve the dark oil for accenting Asian dishes.

Shallot: Though related to onions, shallots look more like giant, brown garlic bulbs than onions. A shallot bulb is composed of multiple cloves, each covered with a thin, dry, papery skin. When selecting shallots, choose those that are plump and firm with no signs of wilting or sprouting. Keep them in a cool, well-ventilated spot for up to a month. Mild in flavor, shallots can be used in the same manner as onions.

Smoke flavoring: Available in liquid form, smoke flavoring is nothing more than smoke concentrate in a water base.

Snow peas: Because the bright-green, thin pods of these delicate peas are edible, the French call them *mange-tout,* or "eat it all." Choose crisp, well-colored pods with small peas, and store them in a plastic bag in the refrigerator for up to three days. Pinch off the ends before using them. Occasionally called *Chinese snow peas.*

Sofrito: Many Spanish and Caribbean recipes call for this thick, flavorful sauce as a seasoning. Traditionally it's made with annatto seeds, pork (or rendered pork fat), onions, sweet peppers, garlic, and herbs. Look for sofrito in jars. Use just a tablespoon or two to pump up any soup that needs a little special character.

Soup: Any combination of fruit, vegetables, meat, poultry, fish, or grains cooked and served in a liquid. Soups can be hot or cold, thick, thin, chunky, or smooth. They can be served as a first course, main course, or dessert.

Spanish onion: A large, mild onion that's in season from August to May. Select Spanish, or "storage," onions that are firm and dry and without sprouts. Store them in a cool, dry, dark, well-ventilated area for up to several months. For longer storage, chop and freeze them.

Sweet potato: Two varieties of sweet potato are commonly available in most supermarkets: a dry type with light yellow flesh and a moist type with reddish-orange flesh. The moist variety is the sweeter of the two and is often mislabeled a *yam.* Look for small to medium potatoes with smooth, blemish-free skin, and store them in a cool, dry, dark place for up to a week. Sweet potatoes are a superb source of vitamin A.

Swiss chard: Sometimes called *chard* and *rhubarb chard,* this member of the beet family has big dark green leaves and large, deep-red or white celerylike stalks. A cruciferous cousin, cooked chard is a powerhouse of vitamins A, C, and folate. When selecting chard, look for crisp leaves and stalks, and remember that a pound cooks down to about a single cup. Store fresh leaves in a plastic bag in the refrigerator for up to 3 days.

Tarragon: An herb popular in French cooking, with a distinctive, almost licoricelike taste. Tarragon's slender, pointed, dark green leaves flavor such foods as chicken, Béarnaise, and fines herbes. Use tarragon with a little caution; its assertiveness can easily overwhelm other flavors.

Teriyaki: A delightful homemade or commercially prepared sauce made of soy sauce, sake (or sherry), sugar, ginger, and garlic. Teriyaki, which has a Japanese origin, also refers to any dish made with a teriyaki sauce.

Thai spice: An exotic blend of chili peppers, ginger, coriander, cumin, cinnamon, star anise, garlic, lemon peel, and dried shallots that may be labeled *Thai seasoning.* Thai spice imparts warm, robust flavor to noodles, rice, soups, and other dishes.

Tortilla: Made from corn *(masa)* or wheat flour, tortillas are thin, flat, round unleavened Mexican breads that resemble pancakes. Traditionally, they're baked, but not browned, on a griddle. Tortillas can be eaten plain or wrapped around a multitude of fillings to create tacos, burritos, enchiladas, tostadas and chimichangas. Pick up prepackaged tortillas in the refrigerator section of your supermarket and store them according to package directions.

Turmeric: Probably best known for the distinctive bright yellow color it gives American-style prepared mustards, turmeric is a musty, bittersweet spice related to ginger. Use this dried powder sparingly; it's pretty intense stuff—so intense, in fact, that it will stain plastic utensils. Turmeric is an inexpensive substitute for saffron.

Watercress: This is a peppery-tasting salad green, which is usually used as an accent. Its leaves are small, dark green, and tender. Choose bunches with well-colored, perky leaves, and store them in a plastic bag in the refrigerator for up to 2 days. To use, discard the stems.

Wild pecan rice: This is a delightful aromatic rice, sometimes labeled simply *pecan rice,* that hails from Louisiana. It has a wonderful nutty flavor, and the grains remain fluffy and separate after cooking.

Wine vinegars: Mildly zesty vinegars made from red or white wines. Use them to make simple vinaigrettes and other salad dressings as well as marinades.

Worcestershire sauce: A dark, pungent condiment made from soy sauce, vinegar, garlic, tamarind, onions, molasses, lime, anchovies, and other seasonings, Worcestershire sauce was first concocted in India and bottled in Worcestershire, England. Use it to flavor soups, meats, gravies, and vegetable juices.

Everyday Equivalents

Recalling most measures—for example, 8 ounces equal a cup and others we use everyday—is a snap. But those used once a decade (at least it seems that seldom) easily slip our minds. To jog your memory and help you measure up, refer to this table of U.S. to metric equivalents, rounded for easy use.

U. S. UNITS			METRIC
LIQUIDS			
¼ teaspoon			1 milliliter
½ teaspoon			2 milliliters
1 teaspoon	60 drops	⅙ fluid ounce	5 milliliters
1 tablespoon	3 teaspoons	½ fluid ounce	15 milliliters
2 tablespoons	⅛ cup	1 fluid ounce	30 milliliters
4 tablespoons	¼ cup	2 fluid ounces	60 milliliters
5⅓ tablespoons	⅓ cup	2⅔ fluid ounces	80 milliliters
8 tablespoons	½ cup	4 fluid ounces	113 milliliters
1 cup	16 tablespoons	8 fluid ounces	236 milliliters
2 cups	1 pint	16 fluid ounces	500 milliliters
4 cups	1 quart	32 fluid ounces	1 liter
4 quarts	1 gallon	128 fluid ounces	3¾ liters

TEMPERATURE		WEIGHT	
32°F	0°C	1 ounce	28.35 grams
212°F	100°C	4 ounces	115 grams
350°F	177°C	8 ounces	225 grams
400°F	204°C	16 ounces (1 pound)	454 grams
450°F	232°C	32 ounces (2 pounds)	907 grams
		36 ounces (2¼ pounds)	1000 grams

Counting Bean Times

You're right. Cooking beans isn't a quick thing to do, but it's not labor-intensive, either. So, when you want legumes with sprightly flavors and low sodium levels to boot, simmer up a batch. The cooking is easy. Soak the beans in water to cover in the refrigerator for 12 hours or in hot water for 1 hour; drain. Cook, using the following table to help you figure amounts and cooking times.

DRIED LEGUME (1 CUP)	COOKING WATER (CUPS)	APPROX. COOKING TIME	APPROX. COOKED VOLUME (CUPS)
Adzuki beans	4	45 to 50 minutes	2½.
Black beans	4	45 to 50 minutes	2½
Black-eyed peas	4	1 hour	2½
Fava beans	4	45 to 60 minutes	2½
Garbanzos	4	2 hours	3¼
Kidney beans	3	1½ hours	2½
Lentils	4	30 minutes	2¾
Lima beans	4	45 to 60 minutes	2½
Pinto beans	3	1½ hours	2
Split peas	3	35 to 40 minutes	2¼
White beans (great northern, navy, pea)	4	45 to 60 minutes	2½ to 3

Winning Ways with Herbs and Spices

A pinch of herbs or spices can do wonders for a soup needing more jazz or a chowder in need of pizzazz. But knowing what seasoning to pair with what food can be daunting even for an accomplished cook. To help you find a good match, here are some classic, palate-pleasing combinations.

<u>HERBS</u>

HERB	FLAVOR	MEAT, POULTRY, FISHES, DAIRY	VEGETABLES
Basil	Pungent licorice	Beef. chicken, lamb, salmon, turkey, tuna	Asparagus, beets, broccoli, cabbage, carrots, cucumbers, eggplant, mushrooms, potatoes, summer squash, tomatoes
Bay leaf	Menthol	Beef, chicken, lamb, most fish	Artichokes, beets, carrots, potatoes, tomatoes
Chervil	Light licorice, parsleylike	Beef, chicken, fish, lamb, shellfish, pork, turkey	Asparagus, beets, carrots, eggplant, mushrooms, peas, potatoes, squash, tomatoes
Chives	Delicate onionlike	Most fish, cheese	Potatoes, tomatoes

Herb	Flavor	Meat, Poultry, Fishes, Dairy	Vegetables
Cilantro	Distinctive pungent smell and taste	Beef	Beans, tomatoes
Dill	Tangy, carawaylike	Chicken, fish, shellfish, eggs, cheese	Avocado, beans, cabbage, cauliflower, carrots, cucumbers, green beans, parsnips, potatoes, tomatoes
Marjoram	Oreganolike	Beef, chicken, fish, shellfish, lamb, pork, veal	Brussels sprouts, carrots, corn, eggplant, mixed greens, peas, potatoes, summer squash
Mint	Menthol	Chicken, lamb, pork	Carrots, cucumbers, green beans, mixed greens, peas, potatoes, summer squash, tomatoes
Oregano	Strong, aromatic, similar to marjoram	Beef, chicken, fish, pork, shellfish, turkey, veal, eggs	Avocado, beans, broccoli, cabbage, corn, cucumbers, eggplant, mushrooms, potatoes, summer squash, tomatoes

Herb	Flavor	Meat, Poultry, Fishes, Dairy	Vegetables
Parsley	Fresh herbal	Beef, chicken, fish, lamb, shellfish, pork, turkey, veal, cheese, eggs	Avocado, beans, cabbage, cauliflower, corn, cucumbers, eggplant, green beans, mixed greens, mushrooms, potatoes, summer squash, tomatoes
Rosemary	Hints of lemon and thyme	Beef, chicken, fish, shellfish, lamb, pork, turkey, veal	Cauliflower, cucumbers, green beans, mushrooms, peas, potatoes, summer squash, tomatoes, turnips
Sage	Slightly bitter, musty mint	Beef, chicken, flounder, halibut, lamb, pork, sole, veal	Beans, beets, brussels sprouts, carrots, eggplant, peas, potatoes, tomatoes, winter squash
Savory	Minty thyme	Beef, chicken, fish, lamb, shellfish, turkey	Artichokes, asparagus, beans, beets, cabbage, carrots, green beans, lentils, mixed greens, peas, potatoes, tomatoes

HERB	FLAVOR	MEAT, POULTRY, FISHES, DAIRY	VEGETABLES
Tarragon	Aniselike	Beef, chicken, fish, lamb, shellfish, pork, veal, turkey cheese, eggs	Asparagus, beets, carrots, cauliflower, green beans, mixed greens, mushrooms, potatoes, summer and winter squash, tomatoes
Thyme	Somewhat lemonlike	Beef, chicken, clams, fish, lamb, shellfish, pork, veal, tuna, turkey, cheese, eggs	Beets, carrots, green beans, potatoes, summer squash, tomatoes

SPICES

SPICE	FLAVOR	MEAT, POULTRY, FISHES, DAIRY	VEGETABLES
Allspice	Combined taste of cinnamon, nutmeg, cloves	Beef, chicken, fish, ham, turkey, cheese, eggs	Beets, carrots, parsnips, peas, spinach, sweet potatoes, turnips, winter squash
Capers	Pungent, briny	Fish, poultry	Spinach
Caraway	Nutty aniselike	Beef, pork, cheese	Cabbage, cucumbers, onions, potatoes, turnips, winter squash

Spice	Flavor	Meat, Poultry, Fishes, Dairy	Vegetables
Cardamom	Gingery–lemon	Chicken, fish, cheese	Beans, carrots, pumpkin, sweet potatoes, winter squash
Cayenne	Hot, peppery	Beef, chicken, fish, shellfish, lamb, pork, turkey, cheese, eggs	Beans, cabbage, carrots, cucumbers, green beans, lima beans, potatoes, spinach, tomatoes
Celery seed	Strong celery	Beef, chicken, fish, lamb, turkey, veal, cheese, eggs	Beets, cabbage, cauliflower, cucumbers, potatoes, tomatoes
Cinnamon	Pungent, bittersweet	Beef, chicken, pork	Beets, carrots, onions, pumpkin, sweet potatoes, tomatoes, winter squash
Cloves	Strong, pungent	Beef, lamb, pork	Beets, carrots, green beans, onions, pumpkin, sweet potatoes, winter squash
Coriander	Lemon–sage	Beef, chicken, fish cheese, eggs	Beets, cauliflower, onions, potatoes, spinach, tomatoes
Cumin	Earthy, nutty	Beef, chicken, pork, salmon, shellfish, tuna	Beans, carrots, cabbage, pumpkin, tomatoes

SPICE	FLAVOR	MEAT, POULTRY, FISHES, DAIRY	VEGETABLES
Fennel	Aniselike	Beef, chicken, lamb, pork, fish, shellfish, cheese, eggs	Beets, cabbage, cucumbers, onions, peas, summer squash, tomatoes
Ginger	Sweet, pungent, peppery	Beef, chicken, fish, shellfish, lamb, pork, cheese	Avocado, cabbage, carrots, summer and winter squash, sweet potatoes
Mace	Mild nutmeg	Beef, chicken, shellfish, veal, cheese	Broccoli, brussels sprouts, cabbage, green beans, pumpkin, spinach, winter squash
Mustard	Sharp, tangy, biting	Beef, chicken, fish, ham, shellfish, pork, cheese, eggs	Beets, brussels sprouts, cabbage, cucumbers, green beans, mixed greens
Nutmeg	Spicy, nutty	Beef, chicken, ham, pork, turkey, cheese, eggs	Beans, corn, eggplant, mushrooms, onions, potatoes, pumpkin, spinach, tomatoes, winter squash
Paprika	Piquant	Beef, chicken, turkey. veal, eggs, cheese	Cauliflower, potatoes, turnips
Turmeric	Musty	Beef, chicken, pork, turkey	Beans, pumpkin, winter squash

Emergency Substitutes

Uh-oh, you've checked the pantry and looked in the refrigerator, so there's no doubt about it: you're out of nonfat sour cream, Italian herb seasoning and chili powder. Three ingredients your favorite recipe calls for, and you planned to serve the recipe tonight. What now? Check this handy table; it'll help you find quick replacements for missing items. Just remember, the substitutes may give the recipe a somewhat different flavor or texture.

RECIPE REQUIRES	QUICK SUBSTITUTE
Bacon (1 slice crumbled)	Bacon bits (1 T)
Allspice	Cinnamon; dash of nutmeg
Bread crumbs, dry (1 cup)	Cracker crumbs (¾ cup)
Broth, beef or chicken (1 cup)	Bouillon cube (1) plus boiling water (1 cup)
Chili powder (1 T)	Hot-pepper sauce (a drop or two) plus oregano (¼ tsp) and cumin (¼ t)
Cinnamon (1 t)	Allspice (¼ t) or nutmeg (¼ t)
Cornstarch (1 T)	All-purpose flour (2 T)
Cumin (1 t)	Chili powder (1 t)
Egg (1 whole)	Egg substitute (¼ cup)
Flour, as thickener (2 T)	Cornstarch (1 T) or quick-cooking tapioca (2 T)

Recipe Requires	Quick Substitute
Garlic (1 clove)	Garlic powder (⅛ t)
Ginger (1 t)	Allspice (½ t), cinnamon (1 t), or nutmeg (½ t)
Italian herb seasoning (1 t)	Basil, dried (1 t), plus thyme, dried leaves (1 t)
Lemon juice (1 t)	Cider vinegar (½ t)
Lemon peel (1 t grated)	Lemon extract (½ t)
Mustard, dry (1 t)	Mustard, prepared (1 T)
Nonfat sour cream (1 cup)	Plain nonfat yogurt (1 cup)
Onion (1 minced)	Onions, dried, minced (1 T)
Pumpkin pie spice	Cinnamon, ground (1 t) plus nutmeg, ground (½ t) and powdered ginger (½ t)
Seasoned bread crumbs, dry (1 cup)	Plain dry bread crumbs (⅞ cup) plus grated Parmesan cheese (1 T) and dried parsley (1 T)
Sherry (1 T)	Sherry extract (1 T)
Teriyaki sauce (1 T)	Soy sauce (1 T) plus powdered garlic (⅛ t) and minced fresh ginger (¼ t)
Tomato sauce (1 cup)	Tomato paste (½ cup) plus water (½ cup)
Vinegar (1 t)	Lemon juice (2 t)

Key to abbreviations: T = tablespoon; t = teaspoon

137

Culinary Math

Quick, quick! A creamy soup recipe calls for 1 cup of broccoli florets. How many pounds of fresh broccoli should you buy? A stew requires 2 cups of beef broth. How many cans should you open? Stumped? That's understandable. After all, who among us memorizes such nitty-gritty food facts? For an approximate answer (it's impossible to be exact), look to this concise table.

A

Almonds, shelled, blanched: ½ pound = 1½ cups whole = 2 cups slivered

Apples: 1 pound = 3 medium = 2¾ to 3 cups chopped or sliced

Apricots, dried: 1 pound = 2¾ cups = 4½ to 5½ cups cooked

Asparagus, fresh: 1 pound = 16 to 20 spears

Asparagus, frozen, cut: 1 package (10 ounces) = 2 cups

B

Bananas: 1 pound = 3 to 4 medium = 2 cups sliced = 1¾ cups mashed

Beans, green, fresh: 1 pound = 3½ cups whole

Beans, green, frozen: 1 package (9 ounces) = 1½ cups

Beans, kidney, canned: 16 to 17 ounces = 2 cups

Beans, kidney, dried: 1 pound = 2½ cups = 5½ cups cooked

Beans, navy, dried: 1 pound = 2⅓ cups = 5½ cups cooked

Beef broth: 1 can (14 ounces) = 1¾ cups

Beef, cooked, cubed: 1 cup = 6 ounces

Beef, ground: 1 pound = 2 cups uncooked

Beets, fresh, without tops: 1 pound = 2 cups chopped

Bread: 1 slice fresh = ½ cup soft crumbs = ¼ to ⅓ cup dry crumbs

Broccoli, fresh: 1 pound = 2 cups chopped

Broccoli, frozen: 1 package (10 ounces) = 1½ cups chopped

Brussels sprouts, fresh: 1 pound = 4 cups

C

Cabbage: 1 pound = 3½ to 4½ cups shredded = 2 cups cooked

Carrots, fresh: 1 pound without tops = 3 cups chopped or sliced = 2½ to 3 cups shredded; 1 medium = ½ cup chopped or sliced

Carrots, frozen: 1 package (1 pound) = 2½ to 3 cups sliced
Cauliflower: 1 pound = 1½ cups small florets
Celery: 1 stalk = ½ cup chopped or sliced
Cheese–blue, feta, gorgonzola: 4 ounces = 1 cup crumbled
Cheese–cheddar, Monterey Jack: 1 pound = 4 cups shredded or grated
Cheese–Parmesan, Romano: 4 ounces = 1 cup shredded or grated
Chicken, cooked, cubed: 1 cup = 6 ounces
Chicken broth: 1 can (14 ounces) = 1¾ cups
Corn, fresh: 2 to 3 ears = 1 cup kernels
Corn, frozen: 1 package (10 ounces) = 1¾ cups kernels
Cornmeal: 1 pound dry = 3 cups uncooked = 12 cups cooked

E

Egg, large: 1 yolk = 1 tablespoon; 1 white = 2 tablespoons
Egg, large: 7 to 8 = 1 cup
Eggplant: 1 pound = 3 to 4 cups diced
Egg substitute: ¼ cup = 1 whole egg; 1 package (8 ounces) = 1 cup
= 4 whole eggs

G

Garlic: 2 medium cloves = 1 teaspoon minced

H

Herbs–basil, cilantro, dill, parsley, thyme: 1 tablespoon fresh, chopped
= 1 teaspoon dried

L

Lemon: 1 medium = 2 to 3 teaspoons grated peel and 3 tablespoons juice;
1 pound = 4 to 6 medium lemons = 1 cup juice
Lime: 1 medium = 1 teaspoon grated peel and 2 tablespoons juice;
1 pound = 6 to 8 medium limes = ⅓ to ⅔ cup juice

M

Macaroni: 1 pound = 4 cups dry = 8 cups cooked
Mushrooms, fresh: ½ pound = 2½ to 3 cups sliced = 1 cup sliced sautéed

N

Noodles: 1 pound = 6 cups dry = 7 cups cooked

O

Okra, fresh: 1 pound = 2 cups sliced
Onion: 1 medium = ½ cup minced = ¾ to 1 cup chopped
Orange: 1 medium = 2 tablespoons grated peel and ⅓ cup juice;
1 pound = 3 medium = 1 cup juice

P
Parsnips: 1 pound = 4 medium = 2 cups chopped
Peas, frozen: 1 package (10 ounces) = 2 cups
Peas, in pod: 1 pound = 1 to 1½ cups shelled
Peppers: 1 medium sweet = 1 cup chopped
Potatoes, sweet: 1 pound = 3 medium = 3½ to 4 cups cubed or sliced
= 2 cups mashed
Potatoes, white: 1 pound = 3 medium= 3½ to 4 cups cubed or sliced
= 2 cups mashed

R
Rice, brown: 1 cup uncooked = 4 cups cooked
Rice, white: 1 cup uncooked = 3 cups cooked

S
Scallions: 2 medium, white part only = 1 tablespoon
Scallions: 2 medium with green tops = ¼ cup
Spinach, fresh: 1 pound = 8 to 10 cups torn
Squash, yellow or zucchini: 1 pound = 3 medium = 2½ cups sliced
Squash, winter: 1 pound = 1 cup mashed

T
Tomato: 1 medium = ½ cup chopped; 1 pound = 3 large = 4 medium
= 1½ cups chopped
Tomatoes: 1 can (28 ounces) crushed = 3¾ cups

Y
Yogurt: ½ pint = 1 cup = 8 ounces

Culinary Abbreviations

t = tsp = teaspoon
T = tbsp = tablespoon
c = cup
oz = ounce
fl oz = fluid ounce

lb = pound
g = gram
kg = kilogram
mg = milligram
L = liter

mL = milliliter
F = Fahrenheit
C = Celsius

Index